Rent from the Land

Rent from the Land

A Political Ecology of Postsocialist Rural Transformation

Johannes Stahl

ANTHEM PRESS
LONDON · NEW YORK · DELHI

Anthem Press
An imprint of Wimbledon Publishing Company
www.anthempress.com

This edition first published in UK and USA 2012
by ANTHEM PRESS
75-76 Blackfriars Road, London SE1 8HA, UK
or PO Box 9779, London SW19 7ZG, UK
and
244 Madison Ave. #116, New York, NY 10016, USA

Copyright © Johannes Stahl 2012

The author asserts the moral right to be identified as the author of this work.

Front cover image "Xha' Miallaq on his mule" © Johannes Stahl

All rights reserved. Without limiting the rights under copyright reserved above, no part of this publication may be reproduced, stored or introduced into a retrieval system, or transmitted, in any form or by any means (electronic, mechanical, photocopying, recording or otherwise), without the prior written permission of both the copyright owner and the above publisher of this book.

British Library Cataloguing-in-Publication Data
A catalogue record for this book is available from the British Library.

Library of Congress Cataloging-in-Publication Data
The Library of Congress has cataloged the hardcover edition as follows:
Stahl, Johannes, 1958-
 Rent from the land : a political ecology of postsocialist rural transformation / Johannes Stahl.
   p. cm.
 Includes bibliographical references and index.
 ISBN 978-1-84331-836-1 (hbk. : alk. paper) – ISBN 978-1-84331-898-9 (ebook : alk. paper)
 1. Land use–Albania. 2. Land tenure–Albania. 3. Rent–Albania. 4. Rural development–Albania. 5. Albania–Economic policy–1992-
  I. Title.
 HD810.5.Z63S73 2010
 333.3'14965–dc22
             2010011709

ISBN-13: 978 0 85728 411 2 (Pbk)
ISBN-10: 0 85728 411 8 (Pbk)

This title is also available as an eBook.

TABLE OF CONTENTS

Glossary   vii

List of Abbreviations and Acronyms   ix

List of Illustrations   xi

Acknowledgements   xiii

Chapter 1. Introduction   1

    The Political Economy of Postsocialist Transformation   4
    Political Ecology and Rent   5
    Access and Access Control   7
    Access Mechanisms in Postsocialism   8
    The Transformation of Value   10
    A Political Ecology Theory of Postsocialist Land Use Change   11
    The Plan of the Book   12

Chapter 2. Albanian Socialism   15

    Isolation, Poverty, Repression and Ideology   16
    Socialist Land Use   18
    From Resistance to Breakdown   22
    Kodra, Bagëtia and Dardha in Late Socialism   24

Chapter 3. Patterns of Land Use Change   29

    The Fragmentation of Land Use   29
    Inter-Village Intensification and Extensification   34
    Intra-Village Intensification and Extensification   39
    Forest Degradation   41

Chapter 4. Unmaking Socialist Agriculture: The Dissolution of Collective Structures   **47**

The Fragmentation of the Plot Structure   47
Impediments to Land Consolidation   54
Changes in Collective Action   62

Chapter 5. Unraveling the Socialist Countryside: Differentiation among Villages and its Effects on Land Use   **65**

The Political Ecology of Land Use in Kodra, Bagëtia and Dardha   66
Factors Differentiating Land Use among Villages   73
Broader Socioeconomic Differentiation among Villages   76

Chapter 6. The Crisis of Capital and Labor: Effects on Land Use within Villages   **81**

The Dependence on Land, Capital and Labor in Agricultural Production   81
The Mechanisms of Access to Land, Capital and Labor   83
Access to Capital and Labor and Land Use Outputs   87
Access Differences among Households   88
Spatial Patterns of Land Use within Villages   93

Chapter 7. The Fate of the Postsocialist Forest   **97**

Albanian Forests after Socialism   99
Peasant Resistance and Custom in Kodra's Chestnut Forests   101
Anarchy and Communal Management of Forest in Dardha   103
Massive Logging and State Corruption in Forests Around Bagëtia   109

Chapter 8. Rent from the Land   **117**

Shifting Rent Dynamics and Land Use Change   117
Rural Transformation and Albania's Accession to the European Union   119

Notes   121

Bibliography   129

Index   135

GLOSSARY

Armiq të popullit	Enemies of the people
Bagëti	Livestock
Copëtimi	Land fragmentation
Dynym	Measure of area for agricultural land. 1 dynym = 1/10 ha
Fis	Kinship group, clan
Furgon	Minibus
Fshat	Countryside, rural area, village
Gorë	Mountain region west of Pogradec
Guri i Kamjes	Table mountain and famous natural monument near Pogradec
IFA	Most popular truck used to haul firewood and timber
Kollonat	Wooden poles, stanchions
Krunde	Bran
Kryeplak	Village headman
Kryetar i komunes	Commune mayor
Kulakë	Formerly wealthy peasant persecuted during socialism
Kullota	Pastures
Lagja	Village quarter, plural *lagje*
Latifondistë	Large landowners
Lek	Albanian currency. In 2004, 1,000 Lek were equal to 8 Euro
Mali i Thatë	"Dry Mountain". Mountain about 20 km east of Pogradec. Also referring to the whole mountain range
Mokra	Mountain region west of Pogradec

Mullar	Cone-shaped pile of hay, straw, or oak branches
Pallat	Modern apartment block
Pleqësi	Council of elders, village council
Qafë Panje	Prominent mountain pass near Bagëtia. The name also refers to the forest located around the pass
Pyje	*Forests*
Raki	Albanian national drink. A strong, clear spirit made from grapes (*raki rrushi*), plums (*raki kumbulla*), or other fruits
Shkolla 8-vjeçare	Elementary school covering grades 1 through 8
Shkumbin	One of Albania's largest rivers
Shoqatë e fermereve	Farmers' association
Shoqëria kursim-kredi	Credit association
Stacion makinash e traktorësh	Machine and tractor station
Tapi	Land title, provisionary ownership certificate
Usta	Pl. *ustallaret*. Master bricklayer
Vatra e kulturës	Cultural center
Via Egnatia	Roman trade route which connected Rome with Byzantium
Vrug	Mildew

LIST OF ABBREVIATIONS AND ACRONYMS

ANFI	Albanian National Forest Inventory
AUT	Agricultural University of Tirana
CFPM	Communal Forest and Pasture Management
DAP	Diammonium Phosphate (fertilizer)
DFS	District Forest Service
DGFP	Directorate General of Forests and Pastures
EU	European Union
FAO	Food and Agricultural Organization of the United Nations
GSHDNJ	Grupi Shqiptar i të Drejtave të Njeriut (Albanian Human Rights Group)
GTZ	Gesellschaft für technische Zusammenarbeit (German Agency for Technical Co-operation)
HPI	Heifer Project International
IFA	Industrieverband Fahrzeugbau (automobile company)
INSTAT	Instituti i Statistikës (Institute of Statistics)
NGO	Non-Governmental Organization
SNV	Netherlands Development Organization
USAID	US Agency for International Development

LIST OF ILLUSTRATIONS

Map 1.1.	The research area in southeastern Albania. Map prepared by Daniel Müller	xv
Photo 1.1.	Plowing with donkeys near Dardha	1
Photo 1.2.	Hitching a ride with loggers	2
Photo 3.1.	Land fragmentation in Kodra	30
Photo 3.2.	Broken irrigation channel in Dardha	31
Photo 3.3.	Terraces and erosion gullies in Kodra	32
Photo 3.4.	Gully erosion in Kodra	33
Photo 3.5.	Trash hotspot near Kodra	35
Maps 3.1 and 3.2.	Land Use in Kodra, 1990 and 2004	43
Maps 3.3 and 3.4.	Land Use in Bagëtia, 1990 and 2004	44
Maps 3.5 and 3.6.	Land Use in Dardha, 1990 and 2004	45
Photo 4.1.	Maliver: Long and narrow strips of land distributed to households in Dardha	51
Photo 4.2.	Discrepancy between distributed land titles and actual land use in Bagëtia	53
Table 4.1.	Land fragmentation in the three villages	54
Photo 4.3.	Distances of a randomly selected household to its plots in Dardha	60
Table 5.1.	Emigration by ethnicity and destination in 2004	73
Table 5.2.	Market access	74
Figure 5.1.	Average household income per village by source in 2004	77
Table 5.3.	Productive assets and general infrastructure per village in 2004	78
Table 6.1.	Household income and land use in 2004	88
Table 6.2.	Household labor capacity and land use	88
Table 6.3.	Production strategies according to household group in 2004	92
Photo 6.1.	Land use of Stiljan and Plaguna Tane from Dardha	93
Photo 7.1.	Gjergji Hoxha loading fir stanchions onto his mule	98

Photo 7.2. An old man from Dardha hauling firewood and fodder
          from the communal forest   107
Photo 7.3. Protected afforestation area in communal forest
          near Dardha   108
Photo 7.4. IFA-truck loaded with poached firewood from Qafë Panje 112

ACKNOWLEDGEMENTS

Writing this book has been an intense journey both literally and figuratively. Along the road, I have met many people who pushed my thinking in fruitful ways. I would like to take this opportunity to thank a few of them here.

First of all I want to express my appreciation to dear friends in rural Albania without whose hospitality, generosity and support I could not have done the field research that was the basis of this book. A warm thank you goes to Lavderim, Arefie, Xhuli, Mira and Landi Çela; Miallaq and Lisa Spirollari; and Jorgji and Plagona Jovani. Thank you also to Theodori Bulli, Dashi Caushi, Namir Çela, Ditor Fraholi, Vasil Jankulla, "*Doktor*" Naum Kitani, Taqo Kitani, and Neim and Tiku Sadikllari.

Furthermore, I would like to thank two families in Tirana who have opened their homes to me for extended periods of time: the Novakus (Qani, Rajmonda, and Mariol) and the Ramas (Hassan, Sanie, Klodian and Bori). I am particularly grateful to "*Mësuese*" Rajmonda Novaku to whom I owe my firsts steps in Albanian. In Tirana, I also want to thank Dr. Fatbardh Sallaku from the Agricultural University for setting me off so expertly in my first study village, and Juliana Shllaku from Citizens' Advocacy Office (CAO) for sharing with me her profound knowledge on the workings of the Albanian land administration. A warm thank you also goes to Gerda Dalipaj, Nebi Bardhoshi and Kuenda Laze for their friendship and plenty of valuable advice. Last but not least, I am especially grateful to my research assistant Klodian Rama who was with me during fieldwork from start to finish. Klodian's dedication, courage and level headedness made him a close friend.

At Humboldt University Berlin, where this book was begun as a doctoral dissertation, I thank the people who collectively composed the Junior Research Group on Postsocialist Land Relations. I am particularly grateful to Thomas Sikor, the Group's leader and my dissertation adviser, for his guidance, encouragement, and enthusiasm. Thomas' standard of academic excellence pushed me to go further and deeper than I might have otherwise thought possible. For fruitful comments, and for their friendship and camaraderie, I also thank the other group members: my research triplets

Ştefan Dorondel and To Xuan Phuc, as well as Daniel Müller, Nguyen Quang Tan, Tran Ngoc Thanh, Tatjana Thelen, Dietmar Richter and Sandra Polsfuhs.

At UC Berkeley, where this book was completed, I owe thanks to the people in the Society and Environment Division at the Department of Environmental Science, Policy, and Management (ESPM). I am particular indebted to Nancy Peluso and Jeff Romm for their readings, insightful comments and institutional support ever since the earliest phases of the writing process. Thank you also to Marco Armiero, Stefania Barca, Gail Hollander, Sang Lee, and Rod Neumann, who all provided helpful comments on individual chapters. Many thanks also to Mary Ann King for copyediting.

Funding for researching and writing this book came from the "Emmy Noether-Programm" of the German Research Foundation (Deutsche Forschungsgemeinschaft, DFG) and from a S.V. Ciriacy-Wantrup Postdoctoral Fellowship at UC Berkeley. I am grateful to these institutions for their generous support.

Finally, at home, my deepest gratitude extends to my wife and companion Dolors Moner Vilanova. Dolors has been a constant source of strength and I am deeply indebted to her for the personal sacrifices she has made while I was writing this book. Last but not least, I dedicate this book to my parents, Inge and Leo Stahl. Without their love this journey would never have been possible.

To all, and to the many others I have failed to mention,

Shumë faleminderit, *vielen Dank*, and a big "Thank You"!

J.S.
Berkeley, California
Summer 2009

Map 1.1. The research area in southeastern Albania. Map prepared by Daniel Müller.

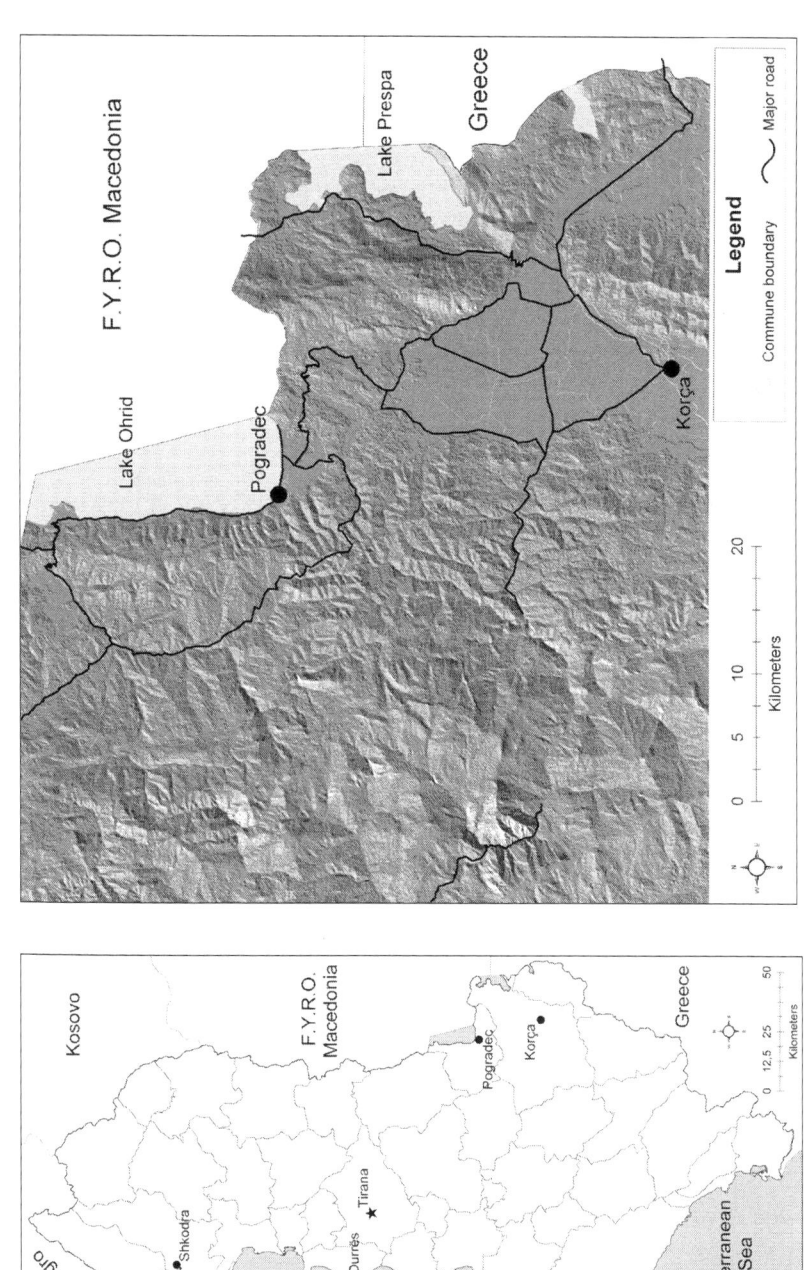

Chapter 1

INTRODUCTION

In October 2004 I traveled from the village of Dardha, where I was halfway through fieldwork, to the village of Bagëtia, where I wanted to conduct a final round of interviews.[1] It was a good day and the journey of 100 kilometers took "only" seven hours. Traveling together with my friend and field assistant, Klodian Rama, I left Dardha when it was still dark at 5 o'clock in the morning on the only bus going to Korça, the central town in southeastern Albania.

Although it was barely fall, the mornings at the foot of the Mal i Thatë mountains were already bitter cold. As the bus bumped over the gravel road, Klodian and I sunk deep into our jackets. Once it was light, I wiped the steamy bus window to see the dry, karstic landscape unfolding in front of us. It was plowing season and people were already out in the fields. Some, it seemed, were

Photo 1.1. Plowing with donkeys near Dardha.

Photo: Stahl.

waiting for hired tractors, while others had taken advantage of the crisp morning air and started plowing with teams of horses or donkeys. To me, it was still striking to see that most people in the fields were women or pensioners. Young men did not work in agriculture anymore.

After two hours of a bone-rattling ride, we rolled into Korça where we hurried to catch the next minibus (*furgon*) to Pogradec. The minibus took us on the national asphalt road and, compared to the regular bus this morning, traveled quickly. The landscape flying by became considerably less dry and evolved into a fertile plain surrounded by high rolling hills. Even on this fertile stretch of land, agricultural plots were small, each less than half a hectare in size. After about an hour on the road, we were forced to stop as horse carts and a flock of sheep blocked the road. We had run into the weekly livestock market at Çerekja where farmers from the whole region come together to trade cattle, sheep and goats.

Just before we reached Pogradec, the driver dropped us off near Kodra, the village where I started fieldwork a year earlier. Walking through Kodra now, Klodian and I postponed several invitations to *raki* (strong liquor) and Turkish coffee for our return from Bagëtia. After a few minutes of chatting in the streets, I flagged down a logging truck that was going up the mountain. We climbed onto the flatboard in the back where the work crew had already taken up the most

Photo 1.2. Hitching a ride with loggers.

Photo: Stahl.

comfortable spots close to the front axle. The men were small-scale, commercial loggers who illegally cut firewood and timber in the Qafë Panje and Guri Nikes forest sector. They knew from experience that the ride was going to get rough. As we exchanged a few words, and Klodian shared his cigarettes, we held on to the planks tightly so as not to be thrown overboard. Over the sound of the growling engine, the crew filled us in on the latest talk from up mountain: who got into a fight with the locals, who was fined by the Forest Service, and who talked himself out of it by bribing an official.

Just as the conversation got most interesting, we reached our final junction. The driver slowed down, and we hopped off at the dilapidated cooperative grain depots at Qafë Panje, a landmark pass above Bagëtia. From the road, we could see the village in the valley below. It was still an hour's walk across extensive mountain pastures to get there, but we made it before noon.

Making this journey fifteen years earlier would have been unthinkable. Albania was still socialist and suffering from one of the world's most oppressive political regimes. Like North Korea today, Albania was virtually cut off from the rest of the world – an island of poverty and demoralization, characterized by extreme food shortages, a moribund economy and crumbling infrastructure. The socialist regime was operating a reign of terror and coercion and controlling internal "dissidence" through surveillance, persecution of extended families, and the widespread use of forced labor camps and arbitrary imprisonment. The regime eradicated private ownership in land and natural resources and nationalized all other means of production. In rural areas, it organized the population in agricultural collectives, restricting rural to urban migration to retain the labor force required in agriculture. In the collectives, rural people were forced into agricultural labor for hardly more than a symbolic remuneration.

In 1991 the socialist regime suddenly fell apart. The collapse was painful and dramatic. For 45 years, the political elites had milked the population for what surpluses it could produce. Now, with the fall of the Berlin Wall and the brutal end of the Ceausescu dictatorship in Romania still resonating throughout the country, Albanians took to the streets and demanded change. Yet, the collapse and the anarchy that followed proved to be only the prelude to the massive political and economic changes that were to shake Albania over the next decade. Stories of mass emigration, political scandal, financial crisis and civil unrest continued to fill the news throughout the 1990s. In urban and rural areas alike, the postsocialist transformation profoundly affected people's lives and their interaction with the natural world. This book tells the story of this transformation and how it became inscribed in the agrarian landscape.

I use the concept of rent as an analytical tool to describe and explain land users' incentives and practices. Rent is the return from control over access to anything scarce and valuable. Viewed through a rent lens, the postsocialist transformation – in Albania and elsewhere in Central and Eastern Europe – altered the mechanisms through which these returns are created and distributed among land users and other actors. I argue that the changes in rent creation and distribution have shifted land users' incentives and productive decisions, causing dramatic changes in land use. The story of my journey from Dardha to Bagëtia illustrates some of these major changes: large cooperative parcels of land became fragmented into tiny, individual plots, former collective farm workers largely withdrew from crop production and invested in livestock or started seeking rent through illegal forest exploitation. In the remainder of this book I seek to subject these and other changes to an in-depth analysis.

The Political Economy of Postsocialist Transformation

Throughout Central and Eastern Europe, the political and economic changes of postsocialism dramatically altered the ways in which rural people use land and natural resources. In the political realm, the postsocialist land reforms brought about massive transformations of land tenure that significantly influenced land use practices. The reforms dissolved socialism's agricultural producer cooperatives and state farms and allocated legal titles to land to smallholders (Swinnen 1997). The new landowners developed a variety of strategies to derive benefits from their newly acquired rights. Some have leased their land to agricultural associations, partnerships, or individual entrepreneurs (Verdery 2003). Many others have become private farmers who make independent land use decisions (Swinnen et al. 1997).

Similarly, in the economic realm, the shift from centrally-planned to market-oriented economies has fundamentally changed the economic conditions of land use. Most postsocialist countries discontinued the "command and control" mode of state procurement in favor of liberalized input and product markets. Domestic and international market liberalization generally created unfavorable conditions for smallholders. Today, farmers face product markets controlled by a few traders and urban speculators (Giordano and Kostova 2002). They have found it difficult to access machinery, obtain agricultural credit, receive extension advice, and purchase inputs (Verdery 1998, 1999; Zbierski-Salameh 1999). As a result, their land use practices often yield low returns. Moreover, much of the value generated in agriculture accrues not to land users themselves but to those who control access to markets, capital, technology, etc. In reaction to these dynamics, many land users have reduced the application of labor and other inputs to land and instituted major shifts in land use practices (Verdery 2004). The shifts have had detrimental consequences including land degradation and negative socioeconomic effects such as decreases in rural income, decreases in employment opportunities, and changes in population size and composition (Miluka et al. 2007).

In Albania, the land reforms and market liberalization have been particularly radical. Albania is the only country in Central and Eastern Europe where virtually all farmland was distributed in equal shares to the former cooperative and state farm workers after socialism (Cungu and Swinnen 1999). The distribution has resulted in the highest degree of individual land ownership found in Central and Eastern Europe (Lerman 2001). Virtually all of Albania's agricultural land is used directly by smallholders and not leased or sold to associations or corporate farms. Land users' choices of how to operate in the new private sector, however, are severely constrained. Albania liberalized domestic markets for agricultural produce and inputs and opened its international borders to movements of goods, capital, and people. As a result, a few, more commercially-minded farmers have to compete against highly subsidized EU production. At the same time, the majority of land users has withdrawn from agricultural markets, turning instead to a mixed approach to farming characterized by a low degree of commercialization and high subsistence production. The constraints faced in agriculture, together with the loss of off-farm employment due to the collapse of state-run rural industries, have caused high rates of emigration and internal rural to urban migration. Since 1991, more than 600,000 Albanians, one fifth of the resident population, have moved abroad. In some areas, emigrants constituted 40 percent or more of the population in 1991. To a large extent, the emigrants originated from the rural areas of the country where they could no longer make a living from agriculture (Zezza et al. 2005).

Taken together, the postsocialist developments in Central and Eastern Europe, and Albania in particular, suggest that changes in the agrarian landscape are due to broader political and economic dynamics that have motivated rural people to alter their land use practices. In this book, I seek to identify the concrete mechanisms by which these broader dynamics have affected land use change in southeastern Albania.[2] Due to the particularly radical nature of its transformation, Albania may not be representative of the conditions commonly found in Central and Eastern Europe, but it is exactly the radicalness of its transformation that makes the effects on land use of political and economic forces more pronounced there than in other countries. Albania is therefore an especially suitable place to study these effects.

Political Ecology and Rent

In order to understand the concrete mechanisms through which political and economic forces drive land use change in postsocialist countries, I adopt a political ecology perspective in which environmental change results from land users' objectives and the constraints imposed on their productive activities by the macro context of political economy. To conceptualize the linkages between land users' productive activities and political economic processes, I examine the creation and distribution of rent among differently positioned social actors. In doing so, I place this study in the tradition of the foundational texts in political ecology (Watts 1983, Blaikie 1985, Hecht 1985, Blaikie and Brookfield 1987).

The concept of rent originates from a branch of classical economics which sought to explain the creation and distribution of surplus profits in agriculture. According to classical rent theory, surplus profits – or "the rents of land" in the words of David Ricardo – are distinct from regular profit because they do not arise from a contribution of land, labor or capital to the production process. Instead, they are created by spatial variations of production conditions brought about, for example, by differences in soil fertility (Ricardo 1973 [1817]) or transportation costs (von Thünen 1966 [1826]). When land is scarce and privately held, the rents of land may be appropriated by landowners in the form of lease payments from their tenants (Ricardo 1973 [1817], Marx (2003) [1894]).[3]

In contrast to the classical conception of "land rent," modern economics suggests that those who control access to any factor of production (not just land) can receive rent due the factor's unique and scarce qualities (von Mises 1961, Fetter 1977). Analogous to the landowner-tenant relationship, rent (in its more general understanding), may be appropriated by all those who control access to anything that is scarce and valuable. Rent, in other words, is created by controlling others' access to production opportunities. It is thus "the benefits levied upon control" (Ribot 1998:314).[4]

Although economic models can identify the quantities of rent available for capture, I seek to comprehend the implications of rent as an aggregate force on social and spatial patterns of land use. I argue that the creation and distribution of rent in its aggregate is a socially formative process, a process that connects the creation and distribution of value and the distribution of power to land users' decision-making and practices. For this reason, one may argue, rent has been a key analytical tool in early political ecology. The extraction of rent from land users by other, more powerful groups has been linked to drought (Watts 1983), soil erosion (Blaikie 1985) and deforestation (Hecht 1985). In their seminal work on land degradation, Piers Blaikie and Harold Brookfield have made the case that rent relations are at the core of environmental change (1987, 19–23). Rent-seeking, they argue, exerts pressure on land users to intensify land use and bring new, inferior land under production. Beyond the optimum point of intensification, land becomes degraded and, as yields decrease, land users become socially and spatially marginalized. In addition to Blaikie and Brookfield's observation, the empirical evidence I present in this book suggests an alternative reaction with similar implications: Albanian land users respond to rent-seeking by other, more powerful actors by de-intensifying land use and shifting capital and labor to non-farm activities, such as employment in domestic or foreign labor markets. The result of this *de*-intensification is often similar to the one Blaikie and Brookfield described for agricultural intensification: Land becomes degraded, as land users cease to maintain terraces or irrigation and drainage systems.

Unfortunately, with a few exceptions (e.g., Guthman 2004a,b), the focus on rent relations, which was so fundamental to early political ecology, has become unfashionable as the field turned to environmental politics in the mid-1990s (e.g., Moore 1993, Peet and Watts 1996, Bryant and Bailey 1997). Yet, as I intend to demonstrate in this book, there is much to be gained from re-discovering political ecology's materialist roots in general, and its focus on rent in particular. I argue that renewed attention to rent as an aggregate force shaping society and environment provides a powerful analytical tool for understanding human-nature interaction in postsocialist contexts and elsewhere.

Access and Access Control

Rent is the return from control over access to scarce resources, so using rent as an analytical tool requires an understanding of the mechanisms through which social actors achieve this control. Two political ecologists, Jesse Ribot and Nancy Peluso (2003), have developed a coherent framework that facilitates this understanding. Defining key concepts for a "theory of access," the two authors suggest a series of "means, processes, and relations by which actors are enabled to gain, control, and maintain access to resources" (ibid:160). These means, processes and relations include legal access to resources through property rights, as well as structural and relational mechanisms that create access to resources through markets, social networks, the institutions of capital and labor flows, technology, social identity, etc.[5]

Applying Ribot and Peluso's framework to the *raki* commodity chain in southeastern Albania provides an illustrative example of the many ways by which actors gain, control and maintain access to resources. *Raki*, the Albanian national drink, is a strong, clear spirit usually made from grapes. Beginning with grape production in the village of Kodra through collection, transport, processing, and trade to final use in the capital (Tirana), first the grapes and later on the liquor pass through the hands of various kinds of social actors, including the grape producers, representatives of a farmers' association, a distillery in Korça, transporters, retail vendors and outlet owners. All these actors are able to capture rent from the *raki* commodity chain, yet the amount of rent they are able to derive and the mechanisms by which they do so differ greatly. Grape producers, for example, control access to vineyards through property rights and are therefore able to retain relatively large shares of the overall rent. At the same time, they must pay rent in the form of membership fees and political support to the representatives of the farmers' association who control access to the distillery, the only large-scale buyer of grapes on market, through highly personalized social ties. The distillery, in turn, captures a significant share of the overall rent due to its control over labor opportunities and marketing. Its control stems from established ties with transporters, distributors, retailers and outlet owners.

The example of the *raki* commodity chain illlustrates the multiple mechanisms that actors employ to benefit from land and other natural resources.[6] Access control is lucrative because it gives actors the ability to mediate the access of others. Subordinate actors must then expend significant resources to gain or maintain access. Access control thus creates rent for those in control while achieving and maintaining access requires a transfer of rent by those who lack control.

Access analyses thus resonate with earlier political ecology studies and their focus on rent relations. In this book, I integrate Ribot and Peluso's framework of access mechanisms into a simple political ecology theory of land use and conclude that access control and access maintenance determine land users' abilities to derive rent from land and other resources. These mechanisms, therefore, affect land users' decision-making and practices. In short, *the distribution of the power to gain, maintain and control access to land, capital, markets, labor and so forth determines the creation and distribution of rent and thus the incentives for land use.*

Access Mechanisms in Postsocialism

One particular insight that the social science literature on postsocialist transformation shares with access theory is the observation that property rights as a mechanism to access resource rents is of less relevance than the proponents of individual private ownership uphold.[7] Like Ribot and Peluso, anthropologists and rural sociologists working in postsocialist countries counter the assumption that exclusive property rights resting in the hands of a single private entity guarantee that the rights holders are able to benefit from their legal title. Early on in the transformation process, Chris Hann has observed that legal access is insufficient without access to other productive resources. Pointedly, he writes:

> "There are many persons and families in Hungary today for whom the current rhetoric about widening choice and extending property rights must seem a sick joke: [...] they cannot become entrepreneurial farmers because they lack the basic capital resources, and their social rights are being whittled away all the time" (Hann 1993a:313).

Property rights, Hann implies, are just one of many mechanisms that actors use to gain, maintain and control access to resources. Examples of alternative access mechanisms include access to markets, social networks, authorities, capital, labor, labor opportunities, and access through social identity.

Access to markets, for instance, is one key alternative. For example in Bulgaria, commercial intermediaries who control access to all major markets are able to extract sizeable rents from land users. Locally known as "sharks", the intermediaries take advantage of farmers' inadequate storage facilities. Often by simply waiting for crop deterioration to set in, they are able to acquire farmers' produce at rock bottom prices (Giordano and Kostova 2002). The difference between the low purchasing price and a fair market price constitutes the extracted rent.[8]

Like access to markets, access to social networks and authority are other key mechanisms providing rent-seeking opportunities for those in control of access. In Hungary, for example, access to social networks and authority have been essential prerequisites for controlling access to agricultural land. Former socialist Hungarian farm managers were able to keep control over land by maintaining collective farms as agricultural associations (i. e. producer cooperatives) under the postsocialist legal environment. In this way, they were in a position to extract substantial rent from association members. The mechanisms that helped managers maintain control were long-standing paternalist relations with the cooperative workforce and an extensive and dependable network of regional and countywide contacts to authorities in the agrarian sector (Lampland 2002).

The rents of land and other productive resources are also determined by conditions of access to labor and labor opportunities. In the deteriorating economies of many postsocialist countries, there is often a surplus of labor, empowering those who control labor opportunities. In many rural areas, however, emigration and a general shift away from agriculture as the main source of residents' livelihoods have led to serious labor scarcity. In Romania, for example, securing labor through social obligations and sharecropping strategies has become increasingly difficult. Often, labor exchange arrangements no longer work, as young people show decreasing interest in agriculture. Labor scarcity is further aggravated by the virtual breakdown of sharecropping arrangements because formerly landless households have acquired land over the 1990s. Thus, Romanian smallholders often face severe labor shortages. Labor scarcity has empowered those who control access to labor, allowing them to capture higher shares of rent than in the past – both in the form of increasing wages for day laborers and higher harvest shares for sharecroppers (Verdery 2003:212ff).

Controlling access to capital (either in the form of financial resources, technology, knowledge or information) is another important mechanism that actors use to capture rent arising from access control. For example, in the early

1990s, the managers of agricultural associations in Romania were able to extract substantial amounts of rent from smallholders who lacked the capital necessary to purchase agricultural machinery. Compelled to turn their land over to associations, smallholders compromised their ownership rights and lost control over production strategies and cash revenue (Verdery 2003:186f).

Finally, access mechanisms are often contingent on actors' social identity. In particular, differences in ethnicity often provide access for some ethnic categories and restrict access for others (Brubaker et al. 2006). Throughout Central and Eastern Europe, legal access to land for instance, has become strongly correlated with ethnic identity. In many countries, privatization laws have deliberately set the baseline date for land restitution in ways that exclude ethnic minorities from landownership (Swinnen 1997). In northern Bulgaria, for example, land rights were restituted only to pre-1944 landowners – effectively excluding ethnic minorities who were forcibly resettled in the region during socialism from landownership (Kaneff 1998).[9]

The Transformation of Value

Access mechanisms are social relationships through which social actors derive value from control over land and other productive resources. The notion of value is fundamental to understanding these mechanisms because, as Caroline Humphrey and Katherine Verdery put it, "no one wants to establish social relationships with respect to things of no value (2004, 12)." To understand the processes of rent creation and distribution, it is important to emphasize that the value of resources is constantly changing, even when the resources themselves remain materially unaltered. As the value of a particular resource changes, the rents derived from control over access to it change as well.

Following Verdery (2003), I see the creation of value as a process which is a function of a context. For example, specific kinds of armshells and necklaces are of immense value only on the Trobriand Islands, yet outside of the Trobriand context, few would ascribe value to these items (Malinowski 1922). Similarly, many indigenous peoples place great value on the unique quality of land as a bond to their ancestors, but the land does not hold this value for urban entrepreneurs. Hence, value is not just the quality of something in relation to prices, it is created in a set of social and political institutions. Any alteration of these institutions necessarily changes value.

Postsocialist transformation is a prime example of radically altered contexts. The transformation period was characterized not only by declining terms of trade for agriculture in almost all countries (Macours and Swinnen 2002), but also by the privatization of collective assets, obligations, risks, and liabilities.[10] Together, the changes in context radically altered existing values. For example, in Romania between 1994 and 2000, incomes and agricultural production costs increased between fifteen- and fortyfold, while the value of land increased only three- to fivefold (Verdery 2003, 208). In a kind of "valuation roulette" (ibid., 23), the values of land, livestock and machinery, as well as the rents derived from control over these resources, were almost entirely up for grabs.

A Political Ecology Theory of Postsocialist Land Use Change

The brief review of access mechanisms and value transformation in postsocialism adds complexity to the simple political ecology theory of land use suggested above. What emerges is a sense of both the diversity of the obstacles actors face and the variety of mechanisms they employ to be able to benefit from land and other resources. The observations of scholars of postsocialist transformation support political ecology's assertion that the mechanisms of access and access control determine the creation and distribution of rent.

In addition, these observations call attention to *changes* in access mechanisms since the collapse of socialism. The political and economic transformations of postsocialism have caused substantial shifts in access, access control, and in the creation and distribution of rent. On the one hand, the land reforms of the 1990s have turned collective farm workers into landowners who have a significant degree of control over land and agricultural implements and are, therefore, able to retain larger shares of rent than during socialism. On the other hand, the changes of the 1990s have been accompanied by new forms of rent extraction from land users. These forms often operate via structural and relational access mechanisms associated with markets, including the examples discussed above (sharecropping, the forced presale of agricultural produce at less than the market price, and exorbitant prices for leasing agricultural machinery).

Finally, the transformation of resource values implies that the rent available to control over access to land and other productive resources is unstable and depends on changing political and social institutions. Access and access control have often become connected to risks and obligations, significantly reducing the rents available for capture.

Taken together, these observations suggest that *since the collapse of socialism, the drastic changes in access mechanisms, the transformation of land and resource value, and the associated shifts in the creation and distribution of rent changed incentives for land use and thus affected land use practices*. As a result, postsocialist landscapes embody the legacy of changes in the creation and distribution of rent in the form of visible patterns of land use.

Using this political ecology theory of postsocialist land use change, I form the following hypothesis about the causes of land use change in Albania since the collapse of socialism: *Changes in access mechanisms and in land and resource value have facilitated shifts in the creation and distribution of rent and therefore altered land use practices in agriculture and forestry, among villages, and among households.* The hypothesis not only suggests a plausible answer to questions about the causes of land use change in Albania, it also justifies focusing on the creation and distribution of rent and their effects on land use change. This focus forms the structure for the remainder of the book.

The Plan of the Book

I carried out fieldwork for this book in several stages between October 2003 and September 2005. Three in-depth village studies conducted during eight months in 2004 form the basis of the study. Except for the winter months, when agriculture is at a standstill, the fieldwork covered an entire agrarian cycle. All told, I conducted 107 semi-structured interviews: 74 with randomly selected households and 33 with key-informants such as village headmen; forest authorities; leaders of farmers', credit and forest users' associations; irrigation workers; former cooperative agronomists and brigadiers; commune staff; and hunters and fishermen. In addition to these interviews, I used direct observation, engaged in countless informal conversations, and conducted participatory mapping exercises with groups of village representatives.

Opportunities for direct observation and informal conversations often arose through my participation in land preparation, harvest activities, and other land use practices in both agriculture and forestry. I also participated in land-related meetings of village councils and farmers' and forest users' associations. Almost always, making contact with people was easy. Naturally, villagers were curious about "their foreigner," and casual conversations were struck up at any given moment. After several months of language training in Tirana and Berlin, I could speak enough Albanian to convey proper respect, a full range of emotions and a sense of humor from the outset. With time, my language skills steadily improved, and Klodian's translation became increasingly unnecessary. In the latter stages of fieldwork, I held most informal conversations in Albanian only.

The book is structured as follows. In Chapter 2, I lead the reader through Albanian socialism up to its collapse in 1991. I focus on socialist land use policies and practices at the national, regional and local levels. In doing so, I introduce the background against which the postsocialist changes discussed in the following chapters will be compared. I argue that the main features molding Albanian socialism – international isolation, deep poverty, extreme repression and an imposed Stalinist ideology – affected all aspects of rural life, including the use of land and other natural resources. I show how these features were reflected in the regime's agricultural and forest policies and how they played out in the practices of cooperatives in the villages of Kodra, Bagëtia and Dardha.

INTRODUCTION

In Chapter 3, I look at what happened to land use in the three study villages after the collapse of socialism. Comparing socialist land use to the practices of farmers today, I identify four distinct patterns:

i. Fragmentation of land use: reflected in the dissolution of large structures built under socialism, such as the cooperative plot structure, irrigation systems and terraces.
ii. Intensification and extensification *among* villages: referring to a shift in land use among villages where the amount of capital and/or labor applied per unit of land has increased (intensification) or decreased (extensification).
iii. Intensification and extensification *within* villages: referring to the intensification of land use in areas near village centers and to the extensification of land use in areas near village fringes.
iv. Forest degradation: referring to a drastic increase in timber and firewood extraction over the past two decades.

In each of the following chapters, I pick up one of the four patterns and explain its causes.

In Chapter 4, I begin by examining the first pattern of land use change (fragmentation). I examine how large collective structures, which were in place under socialism, were dissolved in the postsocialist years. I argue that the fragmentation of land use is the result of broader political and economic dynamics that have caused shifts in the rents available to collective land use.

In Chapter 5, I examine the causes of the second pattern of land use change (intensification and extensification among villages). I argue that since the collapse of socialism three factors have come to differentiate land use among villages: biophysical conditions, market access, and ethnicity. Under socialism, the influence of these factors had been minimized by the economic and social egalitarianism that characterized the regime's strategy for the countryside. After the collapse of socialism, the three factors attained decisive importance because they determined the rent available to land use vis-à-vis other economic activities. They have, therefore, come to shape the production choices of land users within villages.

In Chapter 6, I focus on the causes of the third pattern of land use change (intensification and extensification within villages). I argue that the pattern is the result of a crisis in the supply of capital and labor available to land use. I demonstrate that household production strategies concentrate capital and labor in areas generating the highest land rents. As a result, farmers cultivate areas near the village centers with more labor intensive crops and invest more capital than under socialism. At the same time, they de-intensify production on more distant plots.

In Chapter 7, I examine the fourth and final pattern of land use change (forest degradation). To this end, I trace the quest for resource rent in forests. I argue that with the collapse of socialism the state's grip on forest resources loosened dramatically. As a result, large shares of rent suddenly became available to extra-legal forest exploitation. Consequently, villages have experienced a mad rush on their forest resources that has caused massive forest degradation.

Chapter 8 concludes the book. I summarize the four patterns of land use change and reiterate my argument that the fundamental political and economic changes shaking Albania since the collapse of socialism have deeply affected the creation and distribution of resource rents and therefore caused land use change. I argue that the focus on rent as an aggregate force shaping society and environment provides a powerful analytical tool for understanding human–nature interaction in many resource fields.

Chapter 2

ALBANIAN SOCIALISM

When I first arrived in Albania, I lived in Tirana with the family of my Albanian teacher, Rajmonda. During socialism, she and her husband, Qani, had been part of what in other contexts would have been called the middle-class. Rajmonda had been working as a language instructor at the Agricultural University and Qani was a pharmacist with the military. Surely, their background as educated and relatively well-to-do city dwellers colored the anecdote that Qani told me one evening when we were talking about the life of rural people under the socialist regime.

Years ago, Qani explained, he had been stationed in a remote village near Puka in northern Albania. There, he had heard about a cooperative family who committed an audacious act of insubordination. It was rumored that the family had secretly raised a piglet. Roasted, the little pig was meant to be the highlight of their Christmas celebration. In the early 1980s, this information was already scandalous and dangerous for those involved. Not only was the family obliged to hand over all offspring of their one sow to the cooperative, but celebrating Christmas was illegal because the government had outlawed all religious practices.

There was even more to the story. According to Qani, the family was running a great risk because at times the cooperative leadership sent inspectors to check for the illegal possession of livestock. Those convicted of such acts faced imprisonment in one of the notorious forced labor camps, and their families were "de-classed" (*deklasuar*). Fortunately, the family in Puka had been warned in advance when such an inspector came to visit them. To deceive him, they had made the piglet swallow *raki* until it was unconscious. Then they hid it underneath the blankets in their daughter's bed. When the inspector came to check the premises, he found the young girl in bed sneezing and coughing with the flu. Wary of the germs, he quickly left again without suspicion.

Told in Qani's burlesque way, the little anecdote could lead one to think of Albanian socialism as a farce. Yet, although Qani's account did reveal some of the absurdity of everyday life under the socialist regime, it also contained enough details to reveal some of the most salient features of Albanian socialism: isolation, poverty, repression and ideology. In this chapter, I am going to show

how these features affected all aspects of everyday life, including land and resource use practices in the collective farms.

Isolation, Poverty, Repression and Ideology

Në njërën dore kazmën, në tjetrën pushkë!
In one hand a pickax, in the other a rifle!

Socialist slogan

By the 1980s, Albania not only suffered from one of the world's most oppressive political regimes, it was also virtually cut off from the rest of the world by the vice-like grip of its xenophobic and ultra-centralist dictator of forty years, Enver Hoxha. A former ally of the Soviet Union and the Eastern Bloc, Hoxha split Albania from the international communist movement in 1960 after he denounced his former comrades as "revisionists" who had betrayed Stalin's original principles and now adhered to "Krushchevism." The break with the Soviet Union and the Eastern Bloc left Albania increasingly isolated; China was its last remaining ally. In 1978, two years after Mao's death, Albania also broke with China. Hoxha had openly criticized Mao's successors for the renewal of contacts with the United States and Western Europe. In reaction, China ended economic assistance to its "little red beacon" in Europe, leaving Albania cut off from all foreign aid.

Albania's international isolation only added to the problems of its centrally planned economy. Hoxha's centralist policies refused any devolution of economic decision-making and resulted in a loss of competitiveness, even in the sectors in which Albania had the potential to compete (cf. Saltmarshe 2001). As a result of its international isolation and failing economy, Albania became "an island of increasing poverty" characterized by "extreme, spartan egalitarianism" (Vickers and Pettifer 1997, 12). While food supplies became more insecure year after year, Hoxha blamed the problems on the "savage imperialist-revisionist blockade of the country" (quoted in Pettifer 2001, 89).

The political leadership used Albania's international isolation to conjure up the image of a country being surrounded by hostile powers, including both capitalist and socialist countries. According to Fatos Lubonja, a prominent writer who was imprisoned for "agitation and propaganda" from 1974 to 1991, Hoxha's regime raised people "to believe themselves 'the navel of the world,' a paradise amidst demonic others. […] Both to be at the centre of world attention and to exhibit paranoia about the ambitions of that outside world [with regards to Albania] were integral features of ideological socialisation" (cited in Woodcock 2007).

Hoxha used the image of a nation surrounded by enemies to justify the extreme internal repression that characterized his rule. Repression was the mechanism through which the regime maintained control. The secret police (*Sigurimi*) closely monitored any kind of opposition. Controlling a huge surveillance network, it operated a reign of terror to instill fear among the population. Mass communication was monopolized and used to spread propaganda. In preparation for an anticipated invasion of American, Russian or Yugoslav troops, Hoxha's regime formed a large army that operated underground weapon factories, built 180,000 concrete bunkers, and promoted the construction of millions of concrete poles topped with iron spearheads to impale intruding paratroopers.[1]

As part of the repression, the regime sought to subvert the traditional social structure based on the extended family and patrilineal, exogamous clans (*fis*). It also attempted to destroy religious ties, outlawing religious practices and proclaiming Albania the world's first atheist state in 1967. In almost every village the regime created a pariah class of so-called "enemies of the people" (*armiq të popullit*) who consisted of formerly wealthy peasants (*kulakë*) and deviants from the party line. People who had fallen into this category were publicly ostracized and lived a miserable life. They could access only the most menial jobs and were the last to receive allocations of food, firewood and other necessities. The education of their children was restricted to the elementary level, and anyone who made contact with them also risked being condemned.

Hoxha's regime took the tactics of social exclusion to the extreme through the use of gulags, arbitrary imprisonment, and psychiatric confinement. According to Amnesty International, 18 forced labor camps existed in Albania, which in 1976 contained some 12,000 political prisoners (cited in Saltmarshe 2001, 58). Agim Musta, one of the activists who is most prolific about the crimes committed by the socialist regime, reported that between 1945 and 1992, 5,487 political prisoners were executed, 19,250 people were sentenced to prison, 59,809 people were interned and internally deported, and 11,536 families were banished from border regions to Albania's interior (cited in Woodcock 2007). Given that the population of Albania was less than three million, these figures demonstrate the pervasiveness of the repression that occurred under Hoxha's regime.

To further strengthen its control, the regime combined these forms of repression with the imposition of a particular ideology upon the population. By controlling the dissemination of information through propaganda and restrictions on movement, it played on the population's forced ignorance of political affairs by creating a personality cult of overwhelming proportions that centered around the dictator. Upon Hoxha's death in 1985, the nation sincerely mourned the loss of their national leader and defender. Hundreds of thousands came together in Tirana to pay their last respect to *Xhaxhi Enveri* (Uncle Enver). The signs of grief and mourning that were present throughout the country illustrate that "the regime controlled reason, the minds of people, and their emotions" through its monopoly on ideology (Saltmarshe 2001, 59f).

Socialist Land Use

Luftë për bukën është luftë për socializëm!
A fight for bread is a fight for socialism!
—Socialist slogan on the door of a cooperative grain depot

The four main features molding Albanian socialism – international isolation, deep poverty, extreme repression and imposed ideology – affected every detail of society. As with all other aspects of Albanian life under socialism, these factors fundamentally affected the use of land and resources.

Collectivization

At the end of World War II, before the rise of the socialist regime, the structure of land tenure in Albania was similar to that of a feudal society. Eighty-three percent of the peasantry owned on average 1.8 hectares of agricultural land. At the same time, seven *latifondistë* families each owned 2,000 hectares on average. Between the two extremes, a small middleclass consisted of about 4,700 well-to-do landowners who on average held 19 hectares. In all, of Albania's 2.9 million hectares of land surface, agricultural land counted for 155,00 hectares. Of this some 50,000 hectares were owned by the Albanian state and more than 105,000 hectares were in the possession of the *latifondistë* families and middleclass landowners (Sjöberg 1991, 84).

Hoxha's rural policy strictly followed the Stalinist model by giving priority to the eradication of private ownership. To overcome the inequalities of feudalism, the socialist regime began to steadily nationalize all means of production. In 1945 it initiated the first step towards the collectivization of agricultural land. The Law on Agrarian Reform (dated 30 August 1945) expropriated (1) the land of all landowners employing only hired labor (without compensation); (2) all land in excess of 7 hectares of landowners letting to tenants; and (3) all land in excess of 40 hectares. A second act of the Agrarian Reform (dated 17 May 1946) expropriated (4) all land in excess of 5 hectares per capita; and (5) prohibited land sales (Mathijs 1997, 41f). In total, the Agrarian Reform dispossessed some 8,000 landowners and 480 land-owning religious institutions. About 10,000 other landowners who held more land than the new laws allowed were partly dispossessed (Pettifer 2001, 89). All told, some 300,000 hectares of expropriated land were redistributed to 49,000 smallholders and 21,500 landless rural dwellers (Mathijs 1997).[2]

Redistribution, however, was only meant to be a first step towards collectivization. In 1947, the socialist government created 18 state farms on former Italian agrarian colonies. In 1948, collectivization began with the nationalization of beasts of burden, followed by the nationalization of forests, pastures and water resources (Mathijs 1997).[3] By the 1950s, collectivization had become a mass movement. It was completed in southern and western Albania in 1959. By 1967, private agriculture was eliminated in the mountainous central and northern districts, and the collectivization of the whole country was complete (Sjöberg 1991, 106).

In 1971, strictly adhering to Stalin's principles, the regime began to convert some of the country's cooperative farms into state farms (Mathijs 1997). Individual rights to use agricultural land were restricted to small homegardens of 0.1 hectares in the lowlands and 0.15 hectares in mountain areas. As for livestock, households in the lowland cooperatives were allowed to keep one cow *or* ten small ruminants, and households in the highland cooperatives were permitted one cow *and* ten small ruminants. In addition, the quota for households was one pig, an unlimited number of hens and rabbits, one goose and up to 15 turkeys (Sjöberg 1991, 130).

Agricultural Policy

The regime's agricultural policy considered the profound economic inequality characterizing pre-socialist Albania and sought to create a countryside where rural people became members of agricultural collectives regardless of their economic situation, and where villages would fare relatively equally independent of variation in local socio-economic conditions. Following the Stalinist model, the collectives were subject to a centralized system of state planning and procurement. Based on five-year plans, central planning set the demands on agricultural production. The national level plans were broken down into sub-plans for individual state farms, cooperatives and villages. The production quotas demanded by the plan varied from one agricultural collective to another depending on the regional circumstances. Quotas for cooperatives in the highlands, for instance, were generally lower than those for lowland cooperatives.

State procurement provided the collectives with inputs and took over the delivery of outputs. Inputs and outputs prices were set by the state. For outputs, they differed between compulsory deliveries (i.e. the quantity of agricultural produce demanded by the central plan) and above-quota deliveries. For the latter, the procurement system generally paid higher prices. Output prices also differed between highland and lowland cooperatives. Highland cooperatives, facing biophysical conditions less favorable to agricultural production, tended to enjoy higher prices for their products. Together with the lower quotas for highland cooperatives, this fact explains the 'leveling' of living standards among villages in very different biophysical conditions.

Yet the regime not only set the prices of agricultural in- and outputs, it also subjected both to heavy taxation. This way, it siphoned off economic rent from the collective farms to other sectors of the economy. Initially, the political leadership – again following Stalinist principles – considered heavy industry the driving force of economic development. Therefore, it fed much of the surplus produced in agriculture into the development of large industrial sites such as the monumental metallurgical complex in the city of Elbasan called "Steel of the Party" (*Çeliku i Partisë*). Only after the break with the Soviet Union, did the regime decide to spend more funds for agricultural production and less for industrial production.

The shift from industry to agriculture becomes understandable if one considers that in 1959 Albania still depended on imports from the Soviet Union for 48 percent of its total wheat consumption (Sjöberg 1991). After economic relations between the two countries had ceased, Albania was forced to level the difference. As a result of the shift in policy, the regime lowered input prices and raised outputs prices. The prices for services of tractor and machinery stations (*stacion makinash e traktorësh*), for example, decreased by an average of 19 percent (ibid.). As a result of these measures, the terms of trade for agriculture slightly improved. For the collective workforce, however, the effects were disappointing. Agricultural production continued to fall short of the national plan and, despite an initial rise in incomes from agricultural labor, wages in agriculture remained extremely unsatisfactory to most cooperative workers.

As a logical response to the break with the Soviet Union, the major goal of Albania's agricultural policy was to become self-sufficient in grain production. To this end, the regime started to extend the surface of arable land by terracing, desalinating, providing irrigation, and draining marshes. Through these measures, it doubled the amount of arable land between 1950 and 1989 (de Waal 1995). In order to keep up the necessary workforce to cultivate the newly won areas, the regime relied on a pro-natalist policy that tripled the population in 40 years.[4] In addition, it retained a disproportional number of people in rural areas through the imposition of domestic passports that severely restricted people's freedom of movement. Nevertheless, despite these efforts, Albania still depended on grain imports until the 1970s.

Furthermore, the regime's obsession with self-sufficiency in grain drastically reduced the amount of pastureland (which had been converted into arable plots). In the late 1970s, when Albania had become completely isolated and all foreign aid had ceased, severe shortages in meat, eggs and milk occurred.

The government reacted by further reducing the size of homegardens, prohibiting any form of private market, and forcing peasant families to hand over their remaining livestock to the cooperatives (*tufëzim*).[5] All these measures came under the guise of increasing meat production and eradicating petit bourgeois attitudes but, in fact, they were aimed at increasing workers' labor time in the collective farms (de Waal 1995).

Yet in the face of ensuing food shortages in the 1980s, the regime was also forced to make concessions. In 1985, for example, livestock from the cooperative stock was allocated to the cooperative brigades (*tufza dhe arëza*). Each brigade (i.e. unit of cooperative workers) was then allowed 5–10 cows and a flock of 40–50 sheep and goats. It could allocate manpower to tend its livestock as it saw fit. The proceeds of the small herds could be kept within the brigades and were distributed among its members (cf. Sjöberg 1991). While concessions such as these gave some relief to the hungry and increasingly desperate rural population, they could not still the discontent most rural dwellers felt for the political and economic system.

Forest Policy

The regime's grip on forests was no less tight than on agriculture. Forests were nationalized in the 1950s and controlled and managed by the state. For rural people who had long been dependent on the forest resources surrounding their villages, nationalization meant a loss of customary use rights. To achieve the targets of the central plan, the Directorate General of Forests (*Drejtoria e Përgjithëshme e Pyjeve*), a department of the agriculture ministry, largely pushed aside the fundamental links between forests, agriculture and local communities. Not only did it ignore rural dwellers' dependence on forest resources for food, fodder, employment, and energy, but it also, in effect, broke down the traditional management practices of kinship groups and replaced them with a centrally controlled management apparatus completely out of touch with the economic needs of the rural population.

The central government set targets for the amount of timber to be harvested, wood-utilization standards, forest improvement and reforestation. The supervision of these targets lay with the Directorate General of Forests (de Waal 2004). Its responsibilities included all aspects of forestry including forest administration, conservation and resource extraction. It supervised government-run timber harvesting enterprises and sawmills, as well as paper and fiberboard factories (Meta 1993).

Forest product trade policy was in line with the regime's autarchic ideology. Albania never imported wood products and generated modest income from the export of chairs, plywood and non-timber forest products such as medicinal herbs, essential oils and pine resin. Although the fundamental policy throughout socialism was to keep the rates of felling on par with natural regeneration and planting, forests were overexploited and forest areas reduced. Largely due to the conversion of forest to arable land, there was a loss of 20 percent of forested area between 1959 and 1993.

From Resistance to Breakdown

Ata bënin sikur na paguanin, ne bënim sikur punonim!
They pretended to pay us, we pretended to work!
　　　　　　　　　　—Now popular saying about late socialism

The collectivization of private land, the loss of use rights to forests, the confiscation of privately owned livestock, and the insufficient supply of basic foods led to enormous discontent among the rural population. The rural population tentatively expressed its discontent at first for fear of repression, but it became increasingly undisguised by the mid-1980s. Under socialism, cooperative labor was a largely unpaid workforce. Daily wages were sometimes so low that they were hardly enough to buy a loaf of bread. Albanians today often pointedly summarize the resulting attitude among cooperative workers with the idiom cited above: "They pretended to pay us, we pretended to work!"

Common forms of everyday resistance against exploitation in the cooperatives included foot-dragging and doing the minimal amount of work necessary to avoid reproaches from the authorities.[6] Meanwhile, some cooperative workers devoted their real energies to their vegetable gardens or to tending illegally held chickens and pigs (Vickers and Pettifer 1997). In the oppressive environment of the Hoxha regime, however, many forms of cooperative workers' resistance remained limited to "the language of resistance" (Scott 1985): backbiting, gossip, and assigning rude nicknames.

After Hoxha's death in 1985, Ramiz Alia became his chosen successor. By that time Albania had become an isolated country suffering from increasing poverty and a rapidly disintegrating economy. Alia tentatively suggested some minor reforms, which were mainly technocratic in nature and which resulted in only slightly higher income differentials. While it was clear that Albania was facing major economic problems, the socialist elites were afraid of concessions and reluctant to accept changes. In practice, the essential question of how to modernize the economy was never addressed. Food shortages, low agricultural and industrial productivity, chronic shortages of spare parts, and other technical problems continued to be a heavy burden to the economy throughout Alia's government (Vickers and Pettifer 1997).

During much of Alia's regime, life in the agricultural collectives remained the same as it had been in the final years under Hoxha: agricultural labor with no more than minimal input. Under Alia, the regime steadily lost control, and cooperative workers' resistance grew increasingly outright. In 1987 the party journal *Rruga e Partisë* noted that there had been drastic increases in "pathological social phenomena as parasitism, social anomie and low productivity; an unwillingness to accept assignments in the countryside and remote areas, manifestations of religious beliefs, hooliganism, theft and crime" (Biberaj 1990, quoted in de Waal 1998:26). According to the journal, this "antisocial" behavior took a variety of different forms including corruption, violation of the labor discipline, and theft of cooperative property.

By 1988, the situation of the hungry and increasingly desperate population had worsened to such an extent that open criticism of the government could no longer be suppressed. At the same time, the international context was changing for Albania. Gorbachev's *perestroika* brought fundamental changes to Central and Eastern Europe. Although Albania had isolated itself from the 'revisionist' Eastern Bloc, its stability nevertheless depended on a world socialist presence (Vickers and Pettifer 1997). The mass demonstrations in East Germany which eventually resulted in the fall of the Berlin Wall in 1989, and the brutal end of the Ceausescu dictatorship in Romania that same year, resonated throughout Albania. Afraid of Romanian-style upheaval, the party leadership regarded reforms as inevitable: they freed the press, allowed oppositional newspapers to appear, and permitted oppositional political parties.

The Albanian population, however, would not be calmed down by these measures. People took to the streets *en masse* and demanded change. To the dissatisfied demonstrators, the reform efforts by the government were "too little, too late" (Cungu and Swinnen 1999, 608). Infuriated industrial laborers laid down their work and demanded higher salaries from the state. The strike greatly enhanced the pressure on the regime. In the beginning of 1991, it increasingly lost control over the country. Civil unrest climaxed in the symbolic demolition of the golden Hoxha statue in Tirana on 20 February 1991. In the collapse and anarchy that followed, more than 20,000 people fled to Italy on seized ships, looking for a better future outside the country (Voell 2003). Finally, the Alia government had to agree to the country's first democratic elections, which were held on 31 March 1991.

In the agricultural sector, the combination of a steady crisis in food production and severe droughts (1987–88) signaled the need for a reform of the orthodox Stalinist ideology. In 1988, the government responded by granting some degree of liberalization. On the one hand, it allowed the brigades more self-administration in hopes of better resource-management. On the other hand, it dramatically reduced subsidies to cooperatives and state farms with the intention of improving labor incentives. Furthermore, in order to re-establish a private marketing system for some agricultural goods, cooperative families received between 0.1 and 0.3 hectares of land, and a cow or ten heads of sheep and/or goats (Cungu and Swinnen 1999). All these measures, however, were based on party directives and not on a proper legal basis. By the time the directives reached the countryside, the cooperative workers were entirely demoralized and unmotivated to work for the regime. Resistance had reached its peak. Laborers would only go to work in the cooperatives on special occasions such as the wheat harvest. Theft of cooperative equipment, tools and livestock occurred on a large scale. By 1991, the agricultural sector had virtually collapsed, resulting in a severe hunger crisis that could barely be remedied through international food aid (de Waal 1995).

The final breakdown of the regime in 1991 was accompanied by a frenzied wave of vandalism that shook the countryside. The enraged rural population destroyed irrigation systems, uprooted vineyards and orchards, demolished cooperative buildings, smashed greenhouses, shattered school windows, burned textbooks, tore down cooperative machinery, and ripped out the entire rural telephone system. Although this extraordinary orgy of destruction remains inexplicable to some degree, without a doubt, it delivered a final, detrimental blow to the regime.[7]

Kodra, Bagëtia and Dardha in Late Socialism

The political and economic situation at the village level reflected national developments. In 1990, the year before the breakdown of Albanian socialism, most people in Kodra, Bagëtia and Dardha had long been disillusioned with the regime and were struggling to cope with increasing economic hardship.

Kodra was a large and thriving village in 1990. Located in a fertile valley about eight kilometers away from the regional center of Pogradec, the village had slightly more than 1,000 inhabitants in 312 households. Together with three neighboring villages, it was part of a cooperative that produced a rich variety of agricultural products including grain, forage, fruits, vegetables and tobacco. In addition to crop production, some 200 cows, 250 sheep and several dozens of oxen, horses and donkeys were kept in Kodra. The cooperative infrastructure included three irrigation reservoirs, half a dozen animal shelters, and two large depots to store the harvests. Kodra's enormous fields were plowed, harrowed, and sown using large Chinese caterpillar tractors which the cooperative rented from a state-owned machinery station. Workers brought in grain with combine harvesters, rented from the same station. In response to the regime's doctrine of self-sufficiency, the cooperative tried to keep even the most remote and unproductive mountain pastures under cultivation. To this end, it constructed terraces and an extensive irrigation and drainage system on the valley slopes. Of the six cooperative brigades in Kodra, two tended to wheat, corn and tobacco, while the others were responsible for fruit trees, grape vines, livestock and construction. Each brigade counted between 50 and 80 workers.

In Bagëtia, the infrastructure was similar to that of Kodra – although Bagëtia was much smaller. Located in the rugged *Gorë* Mountains amidst immense old-growth forests and mountain pastures, it was home to 350 people in 70 households. The people of Bagëtia identified themselves as Vlachs (*Çobenj*), an ethnic category comprised of people who spoke a Romance language and who had traditionally been transhumant shepherds (Winnifrith 1987).[8] Although Bagëtia's mountainous terrain was not suitable for crop production, central planning required the cooperative – consisting of Bagëtia and two other (ethnic Albanian) villages – to produce wheat, rye and corn. Each year the three villages had severe difficulties meeting the production quotas set by the Ministry of Agriculture. Livestock husbandry, producing meat, wool and dairy products, had to make up for the low productivity in crop production.

Yet despite these difficulties, Bagëtia and the other two villages were on relatively equal footing with cooperatives with better biophysical conditions. This was mainly a result of the massive support state procurement provided to crop cultivation in form of machinery services and inputs. In addition, the regime invested in the villages' infrastructure despite their remote locations. A road connected Bagëtia to the lowlands, and the village also had a cultural center, an elementary school, a store selling consumer goods, a small irrigation system, livestock shelters, and two large grain depots. Adult laborers worked in cooperative brigades and engaged in small-scale household production just like their peers in Kodra.

In Dardha, like in Bagëtia, people belonged to an ethnic minority. Dardha was one of nine Macedonian villages located on the Albanian side of the Prespa Lakes.[9] Compared to the other eight Macedonian settlements, it was a relatively new village. Founded in the late 18th century, its development picked up speed with the rise of the socialist state. Shortly after Dardha had been collectivized in 1956, it became a cooperative center that attracted the residence of many of the cooperative leaders from the nearby villages. As a result of its successful development, Dardha had a population of 340 people in 79 households in 1990. The village excelled in agricultural productivity. It controlled more than 100 hectares of fields and pastures of which about 60 hectares were irrigated. Dardha's people cultivated mainly wheat and corn in a cooperative they had formed together with the inhabitants of surrounding villages. Starting in the early 1980s, they also raised a growing herd of livestock, which by 1990, included some 90 heads of cattle, 250 sheep, 800 goats and more than 100 draft animals. In addition, the village kept some 1,000–2,000 chickens in a battery farm. A book about the Prespa region, therefore, lauds Dardha because "the duties of the plan were realized [...] in agriculture and livestock, and even more was produced" (Apostoli 2002, 43).

Despite this strong economic performance, Dardha did not stand out among other Southeastern Albanian villages in terms of amenities. In fact, Dardha's infrastructure was comparable to that of Bagëtia: Dardha had a cultural center, an elementary school, a cistern for storing drinking water, an irrigation system, stores selling consumer goods, shelters for livestock, and grain depots. The only significant difference was the chicken farm in Dardha, for which there was no equivalent in Bagëtia. Otherwise, most of the villagers worked in the one of the three cooperative brigades, cultivated small household plots, and raised some animals on their own.

This brief review of the situation in Kodra, Bagëtia and Dardha in 1990, demonstrates the economic and social egalitarianism that characterized the regime's strategy for the countryside. The strategy had its roots in the distinct features characterizing Albanian socialism. International isolation, poverty, extreme repression and a Stalinist ideology created a countryside where rural people became members of agricultural cooperatives regardless of their economic situation, and where villages fared equally well independent of any variation in local conditions.

Although Kodra, Bagëtia and Dardha were inhabited by three different ethnic groups (Albanian, Vlach and Macedonian), the social differences among them were relatively modest. They were modest because despite the diversity of these groups, the socialist regime had sought to downplay the distinctiveness of their cultures and histories (cf. de Rapper 2005). In the regime's perception, national unity was critical for developing a strong Albania that could withstand foreign invasion. The regime thus emphasized membership in the Albanian nation regardless of ethnic identities and promoted a singular national identity by instituting a one-language policy and systematically integrating ethnic minority representatives into the political system (GSHDNJ 2003).

Just as the regime's social policy served to downplay ethnic distinctions, its agricultural policy sought to diminish economic differences. In terms of land use, the differences among villages were relatively small because of central planning, state procurement, and investments into the rural infrastructure. Considering the profound inequality characterizing pre-socialist Albania, the regime's strategy to even out social and economic differences among rural dwellers "worked" in the sense that it created a relatively homogenous society, albeit one homogenized at an extremely low level of socioeconomic development.

To some extent, the situation in Kodra, Bagëtia and Dardha reflected the broader rural experience in socialist Central and Eastern Europe.[10] Land had become socialist property through confiscation and collectivization; agricultural production was centrally planned and organized in state farms and cooperatives; a state procurement system provided the agricultural producers with inputs and distributed outputs; the amount of land left aside for private subsistence production was minimal; and low wages and hardship in a "shortage economy" led to enormous discontent and hidden forms of resistance that contributed to the breakdown of the socialist system.[11] Because the experience in the three villages was analogous to much of the rural experience in Central and Eastern Europe, a closer look at land use change in the three villages after the collapse of socialism may therefore provide opportunities for insights into the broader dynamics of land use change in Albania, Central and Eastern Europe, and postsocialism in general.

Chapter 3

PATTERNS OF LAND USE CHANGE

Since the collapse of socialism, land use has changed dramatically in Albania. When I first visited the country in 2003, one of the more obvious changes jumped out at me before I had even set a foot on Albanian soil. As the plane descended upon Rinas Airport outside of Tirana, I was struck by the mosaic of agricultural plots that came into sight. This vast area of cropland in its mix of warm colors, stood out among the settlements and wooded hills. As we descended further, I could identify individual houses, cars and even haystacks. It was then that I realized how tiny these plots were. Some, I figured, did not measure more than maybe 100 square meters. This observation was even more striking because, in preparation for my visit, I had read Örjan Sjöberg's (1991) essential book on socialist rural Albania, in which he describes the functioning of mechanized, industrial agriculture on large cooperative parcels.

The fragmentation of the collective plot structure that so struck me, however, was just one of many land use changes that occurred after the collapse of socialism. In this chapter, I provide a basic description of these changes and classify them into four distinct patterns: fragmentation of land use, inter-village intensification and extensification, intra-village intensification and extensification, and forest degradation. The following four chapters will examine each pattern, and the forces driving each pattern, in detail. The evidence I present in this chapter is based on satellite images and other visual observations made in 2003 and 2004 (Pattern I); productivity data obtained mostly from the agricultural offices of the communes (Pattern II), participatory land use maps for 1990 and 2004 (Pattern III)[1], and statistics from the District Forest Service of Pogradec (Pattern IV).

The Fragmentation of Land Use

The first pattern of postsocialist land use change that I identify is the "fragmentation of land use." By "fragmentation" I mean the dissolution of large physical structures which were in place during socialism. I will now flesh out this first pattern in Kodra, Bagëtia and Dardha and demonstrate that it reflects broader changes at the national level.

Photo 3.1. Land fragmentation in Kodra.

Source: QuickBird™-Image 04-30-2003.

Plot Structures

After the collapse of socialism, the large parcels of Albania's collective farms were split into approximately 1.8 million small plots (Ministry of Agriculture and Food 2002). This national trend was reflected in the fragmentation of plot structures in Kodra, Bagëtia and Dardha. The cooperatives, of which the three villages had been a part, operated on immense parcels, frequently measuring up to 15 hectares. Compared to these units, the plots of farmers in 2004 were extremely fragmented. The changes are clearly evident in satellite images from 2003 which show the contours of the former cooperative parcels and display their fragmentation into small, individual plots (see, for example, Photo 3.1).

Irrigation Systems

The construction of irrigation and drainage systems had been a priority under the socialist regime. At the end of the 1980s, more than 420,000 hectares of agricultural land in Albania were irrigated. The destruction of irrigation facilities in the upheaval of the system change caused the irrigated area to plummet to 340,000 hectares (Food and Agricultural Organization 2006).[2]

Photo 3.2. Broken irrigation channel in Dardha.

Photo: Stahl.

The changes in the irrigation infrastructure at the national level were mirrored in developments in the three study villages. After the collapse of socialism, irrigation systems were dismantled in Bagëtia and Dardha (see Photo 3.2). Only in Kodra had the irrigation system remained partially functional. Yet, even there, one of its three cooperative water reservoirs was inoperative.

Terraces

Cooperative terraces had been constructed under socialism to bring new land under cultivation. After the system change, they largely deteriorated. As a result, soil erosion on terraced land became a serious problem for the three villages (see Photo 3.3).

By 2004, it was clear that, compared to socialist times, erosion resulting from the overuse of terraced land had increased. Although overuse of terraces had also occurred in the cooperatives, its effects were mitigated largely by strictly controlling water runoff through irrigation and drainage channels. By 2004, erosion most often occurred on formerly terraced land or along roads and paths overused by human activities or livestock (see Maps 3.2 and 3.6).

Photo 3.3. Terraces and erosion gullies in Kodra.

Source: QuickBird™-Image 04–30–2003.

PATTERNS OF LAND USE CHANGE   33

On slight inclines in the relief, running water then wore away the land surface. Erosion was most severe in Kodra and Dardha and generally occurred through gully erosion, although sheet erosion was also common (see Photo 3.4). The negative consequences of soil erosion included not only the degradation of

Photo 3.4. Gully erosion in Kodra.

Photo: Stahl.

fertile arable land, erosion had also increased sedimentation in the rivers, streams and lakes of the watershed.

Waste Disposal

The system of waste disposal, like irrigation, underwent dramatic changes since the collapse of socialism. The socialist regime had paid little attention to environmental issues such as the disposal of industrial or agricultural wastes. For example, the proliferating aluminum, ferrous-nickel, chromium and coal mines on the Albanian side of Lake Ohrid severely contaminated the watershed. Although most of these mines were closed after the system change, the contamination persisted because the mines had piled large amounts of rock wastes along streams and at the shore of the lake.

In postsocialism, the problems associated with waste disposal became even more severe. For example, agricultural intensification in some areas and the sudden and widespread availability of detergents and different kinds of plastic materials led to contamination of the watersheds. As a result, natural habitats along creeks and ponds deteriorated. The increasing use of detergents led to serious phosphor pollution in many water bodies.

The general problems associated with waste disposal in Albania were reflected by negative trends in Kodra, Bagëtia and Dardha. In all three villages, fecal contamination of the watersheds was extremely high. None of the villages had a sewage system, and human and animal waste usually infiltrated directly into the soil. Only in Dardha were (some) dung piles lined with concrete to prevent infiltration. A public garbage collection service did not exist. Informally, certain areas in each village had developed into trash spots where solid waste was dumped. Often, sewage, solid and hazardous wastes were disposed of in streams or irrigation reservoirs (see Photo 3.5).

Inter-Village Intensification and Extensification

I now turn to the second pattern of land use change, "inter-village intensification and extensification," a pattern that describes spatial changes at the regional level and reflects changes in the intensity of land use among villages. By "intensification" I mean a shift in land use where the amount of capital and/or labor applied per unit of land increases. By "extensification" I refer to a shift in land use where the amount of capital and/or labor applied per unit of land decreases. In the following, I will look at this pattern across the three study villages, using statistical data on agricultural productivity and inputs to make determinations about increases and decreases in the amount of capital and labor applied.

Photo 3.5. Trash hotspot near Kodra.

Photo: Stahl.

Intensification in Kodra

By 2004, land use in Kodra differed markedly from 1990. Farmers cultivated their small private plots with a variety of vegetables, grapes, fruit, and alfalfa. Unlike in many Albanian villages, the irrigation infrastructure in Kodra was still largely functional. Two water reservoirs irrigated about 50 hectares of fields used for intensive cultivation.

Compared to the socialist period, grain production in Kodra had declined dramatically. The surface area grown with wheat had fallen from 50 hectares in 1990 to 5 hectares in 2004.[3] Similarly, the surface on which corn was grown declined from 20 to 10 hectares. Wheat and corn were planted almost entirely as feed for livestock.[4] The surface area released from grain production was planted with more labor intensive crops, such as fruits and vegetables, than it used to be under the cooperative. During socialism the irrigated land had yielded only one harvest per year (wheat or corn in rotation), but now it was often cultivated twice a year – first with grain (for forage) and then with vegetables.

By 2004, grapes and onions had become the most important cash crops in Kodra. The productivity of grapes had increased more than three fold since 1990, mainly because of the introduction of Diammonium Phosphate fertilizer (DAP) and the rejuvenation of the old rootstock with Riesling, Tokaj and Muskat varieties. Regarding livestock, the number of cattle, sheep and goats had increased. The number of cattle had risen from 200 head in 1990 to 300 in 2004. The number of sheep and goats had increased from 250 to 900. In addition to increasing livestock numbers, Kodra's farmers association had introduced new, more productive breeds in about 10 percent of all households. The new Holstein and Bruna Alpina cows, for example, produced about 5 times more milk than the regular Jersey crossbreeds. Thus, compared to cooperative times, livestock had increased not only in number but also in productivity.

Extensification in Bagëtia

As in Kodra, land use in Bagëtia in 2004 differed greatly from 1990. Yet, unlike in Kodra, land use in Bagëtia had not become more intensive. To the contrary, villagers had largely abandoned agricultural production. Crop production, in particular, declined by more than 97 percent since 1990. By 2004, the main objective of agricultural activity in the village was the production of winterfeed for the villagers' livestock.

Alfalfa, hay and the leaves of oak branches made up the bulk of forage used in winter. The little wheat, corn and rye still grown was used mainly for straw and silage. Potatoes and sugar beets were used to feed newly introduced pigs.

Like the number of crops, the number of livestock had declined considerably. Since 1990 cattle had fallen from 80 heads to 28. The number of sheep and goats had declined from 1,300 to 480. The number of horses, mules and donkeys had declined from 110 to 20. Only pigs had increased from zero in 1990 to 18 in 2004.

As the comparison of production figures demonstrates, agricultural land use in Bagëtia had plummeted by 2004. For the little plowing that occurred, the men used horses or mules. Agricultural machinery was not available. Hardly any of the cooperative infrastructure was left intact: the irrigation channels were overgrown and hardly visible in the landscape; and the livestock shelters and the cultural center had been destroyed during the breakdown of 1991. Only the large grain depots at Qafë Panje were still in use, though not for grains storage, but rather as one of the most spacious livestock shelters in the district of Pogradec.

Extensification in Dardha

Like in Bagëtia, after the collapse of socialism, the intensive production of the cooperative in Dardha gave way to a much more extensive kind of land use. By 2004, people in Dardha produced their crops almost entirely for household consumption. They still rotated wheat and corn on their fields, but rather than being processed to flour, the crops were used to provide straw and forage as winterfeed for livestock. Thus, while the surface area for grain production remained constant, productivity had decreased. Wheat had fallen from 25 quintals/ha in 1990 to 23 quintals in 2004. For corn, the decrease had been even more pronounced: from 35 to 13 quintals/ha.

Behind wheat and corn, grapes had become the most important crop in Dardha. Between 1990 and 2004, the surface area cultivated with grapes had grown from 14 to 19 hectares. The increase reflected the introduction of DAP fertilizer and increased application of phosphates from 45 to 184 kg/ha.

The number of domestic animals in Dardha had decreased as well, except for cattle. While the number of sheep and goats fell from over 1,000 heads to 230, the number of cattle increased from 90 to 200. The rise in cattle may be explained by the simple fact that the collective cattle herd was kept in the neighboring village in 1990 while the only cows in Dardha were those of households and brigades.

A Pattern of Land Use Change Among Villages

Comparing the production figures for grain, fruits, vegetables and livestock in the three villages yields a clear pattern of inter-village land use change.

On the one hand, intensification had occurred in Kodra where crop cultivation had given way to the production of vegetables and dairy products. On the other hand, extensification was discernible in Bagëtia where all agricultural activities had dramatically decreased. Positioned between the two extremes, Dardha had also experienced a process of extensification, albeit not nearly as rigorously as in Bagëtia. Wheat and corn production in Dardha had remained relatively stable in terms of total surface area but decreased in productivity per unit of land. Only the productivity of grapes had increased. The number of livestock (except cattle) had fallen dramatically. Thus, while the trend of extensification in Dardha was not as pronounced as it was in Bagëtia, a decrease in overall productivity was still clearly observable.

I identified this pattern of inter-village intensification and extensification by analyzing the villages' production figures, and the pattern can be corroborated by examining the changes in inputs to agricultural production. In Kodra, the irrigation system had largely remained intact, the quality and quantity of fertilizer input per unit of land increased, and the labor input per unit grew. In Bagëtia, on the other hand, the irrigation infrastructure was allowed to fall into disrepair and the use of chemical fertilizers, tractors and other agricultural machinery was abandoned. With an almost exclusive focus on animal husbandry, the input of labor per unit of land in Bagëtia decreased drastically. Finally, in Dardha, although the quality of chemical fertilizer improved and wheat and corn production remained highly mechanized, the irrigation system was dysfunctional and the input of labor per unit of land had decreased.

The changes in Kodra, Bagëtia and Dardha reflected a broader trend in Albanian agriculture. At the national level, grain production had deceased dramatically, just as it did in the three study villages. By the end of the 1990s, for example, Albania – once largely self-sufficient in wheat – produced only 40–50 percent of the wheat it consumed (about 300,000 tons produced vs. 700,000 consumed) (Kodderitzsch 1999, 3). While grain production plummeted, cash crops like grapes and vegetables displayed a different dynamic. After an immediate decline of grape production after the system change, production began to increase again since the mid-1990s (Food and Agricultural Organization 2006). Finally, livestock and dairy production increased drastically, particularly in the early 1990s (ibid.). In the less fertile highlands, where animal husbandry had a clear comparative advantage, livestock and dairy production largely replaced cereal production (Kodderitzsch 1999, 4). The inter-village intensification and extensification established in the three study villages is therefore reflective of postsocialist land use change across Albania.

Intra-Village Intensification and Extensification

The third pattern of land use change, "intra-village intensification and extensification," refers to changes in land use intensity that have occurred within villages. To describe the pattern, I compare the changes in land use within Kodra, Bagëtia and Dardha using the participatory land use maps of 1990 and 2004 (Maps 3.1–6). I suggest that land use in areas closer to village centers has become more intensive, while in areas closer to the village fringes, it has become more extensive.

Land Use Change within Kodra

Kodra is located in a valley which is divided by an asphalt road running east to west. To the south of the road, below sharply rising hills, the village is bordered by a small creek. Somewhat more gentle slopes lie to its north. The most intensive types of land use in Kodra – in 2004, as during socialism – occurred at the valley bottom. The cooperative had planted wheat, corn and tobacco there. By 2004, a sizeable part of this land had undergone significant intensification, especially the areas closest to the village center where onions and other vegetables were grown (see Maps 3.1 and 3.2).

Moving up from the slopes of the valley, land use had become less intensive compared to socialism. In 2004, the steep southern slopes were used almost entirely as common pasture. In 1990, they had been cultivated with wheat. On the more gentle northern slopes, cropland had been turned into pasture except for 45 hectares which had been planted by the cooperative.

In late socialism, Kodra's territory had contained five large patches of fruit trees, two on the northern slopes of the valley and three on the southern slopes. Primarily apple, plum, and cherry trees were planted in these areas. After 1990, land use in these areas became less intensive as well. For example, the trees in the northernmost area were cut and turned the area into pasture. Overall, the cooperative had harvested about 2,000 quintals of apples and 400 quintals of plums per year. By 2004, the old cooperative trees had passed their productive climax and production had plummeted.

Land Use Change within Bagëtia

Bagëtia is located at the confluence of two small creeks in the southeastern corner of a vast, mountainous territory. To irrigate the cropland northwest and southeast of the village, the cooperative had supplemented the two little streams with simple irrigation channels. The non-irrigated cropland to the South had been planted with the same crops, corn and wheat. The lack of irrigation had been less of a problem for wheat, but corn production figures had fluctuated greatly depending on the annual amount and distribution of rainfall. The cooperative had used the more remote and steep cropping areas (such as the five "fingers" to the north of the village) for the relatively extensive, non-irrigated production of wheat, barley and rye.

By 2004, the cropland around Bagëtia had shrunk to a tiny fraction of its original size (see Maps 3.3 and 3.4). Located just outside the village to the South, the area was used mainly to grow alfalfa – interspersed with an occasional corn or wheat field or wild plum and apple trees. The abandoned cropland had been turned into pasture. Fruit trees still existed in the small area southeast of the village where they had been planted by the cooperative.

Land Use Change within Dardha

Dardha is locked between Lake Prespa to the east and the *Mal i Thatë* mountain range to the west. The gravel road from the Macedonian border to the Albanian city of Korça runs generally in a north-south direction parallel to the lakeshore (see Maps 3.5 and 3.6).

By 2004, Dardha had experienced a noticeable decrease in cropland. Most of the remaining cropland lay close to the village along both sides of the road. During socialism, the later abandoned cropland had been irrigated through a complex system of irrigation and drainage channels. The channels were destroyed in the upheaval of the system change and, since then, not replaced. Without irrigation, this land became too unproductive for farmers to continue cultivation.

While cropland was thus used less intensively 2004 than in 1990, the cultivation of grapes had intensified. The terraces of the vineyards were maintained, and, as described in the previous section, grape production figures had increased. Moreover, some 2.5 hectares of former cropland had been converted into vineyards.

A Pattern of Land Use Change within Villages

My examination of the land use changes within the three villages reveals a third pattern of land use change: land use within Kodra, Bagëtia and Dardha has become more intensive at the village centers and less intensive at the village fringes in the postsocialist period.

The pattern of intra-village intensification and extensification was most clearly evident in Kodra where grain production had been replaced by intensive vegetable production in the area closest to the village center. In a second ring around the village center, farmers had planted corn and alfalfa in place of the cooperative's wheat and corn rotation. Finally, in a third ring, cropland had been abandoned and turned into pasture.

The pattern is also discernible in Bagëtia and Dardha. In Bagëtia the area that was still most intensively used was located just outside the village center. At distances further away, cropland had been turned into pasture. In the same way, in Dardha, most cropland that was still in use was located around the village center and cropland turned into pasture lay at the village fringes. There was only one exception to this general pattern. Viticulture – typically located closer to the village fringes – had undergone pronounced intensification.

Forest Degradation

Finally, the fourth pattern of land use change in postsocialist Albania occurred in the country's forests. Since the collapse of socialism, Albanian forests have suffered from severe degradation. According to Agrotec's Albanian National Forest Inventory (ANFI), the country's forests declined from 26 percent of the total land surface in 1991 to 22 percent in 2001.[5] However, as I indicate in Chapter 7, actual forest degradation may be significantly higher than the national forest cover data suggests.

The dramatic change in forest quality and cover at the national level was reflected in the forest dynamics of Kodra, Bagëtia and Dardha. I discerned the dynamics at the village level by comparing the land use maps of 1990 and 2004, and by examining the production figures in the forest areas around the villages.

In Kodra, old-growth forest and coppice consist primarily of either oak or chestnut species.[6] While the oak forest had not undergone significant changes since 1990, the chestnut forest had been largely destroyed. Of Kodra's four original chestnut patches, only one in the easternmost corner of the village territory remained productive (see Maps 3.1 and 3.2).

Bagëtia had always been much richer in forest resources than Kodra. The village territory lies in the Qafë Panje and Guri Nikes forest sector, which encompasses some 4,000 hectares of valuable old-growth forest. By 2004, this forest had become significantly degraded, as Maps 3.3 and 3.4 illustrate. The ongoing degradation was reflected in the dramatic increase in the wood volume extracted in Qafë Panje and Guri Nikes. According to Ylli Gallo, the former director of the District Forest Service in Pogradec, the volume of extracted timber and firewood had increased from 35,000 cubic meters in 1990 to 55,000 cubic meters in 2004.

Finally, in Dardha, forests had undergone significant degradation, just as in Kodra and Bagëtia. By 1997, nearly 262 hectares of Dardha's valuable old-growth forest had turned into shrub and coppice (see Maps 3.5 and 3.6). Forest degradation in Dardha was also reflected in firewood and timber extraction figures. According to Rako Dautovski, the head of the communal forest user association, 2,000 cubic meters were extracted in Dardha in 1990. After the collapse of socialism, extraction had jumped to 3,500 cubic meters in 1995 and peaked at 5,000 cubic meters in 1997. Since 1997, the volume extracted remained at about 500 cubic meters annually.

Overall, the severe degradation of forest resources in Kodra, Bagëtia and Dardha provides evidence of a larger pattern of forest degradation. The extraction of timber and firewood drastically increased in the post-socialist period and reached highly unsustainable levels.

In sum, I have described in this chapter land use changes in three villages in southeastern Albania since the collapse of socialism. By comparing socialist land use in 1990 to the practices of farmers in 2004, I have identified four distinct patterns of land use change. In the following four chapters, I will examine the causes of each of these patterns by drawing on in-depth case studies from Kodra, Bagëtia and Dardha. My analysis will focus on shifts in land users' practices brought about by changes in rent creation and distribution resulting from the broader political and economic dynamics of postsocialism.

Maps 3.1 and 3.2. Land Use in Kodra, 1990 and 2004.

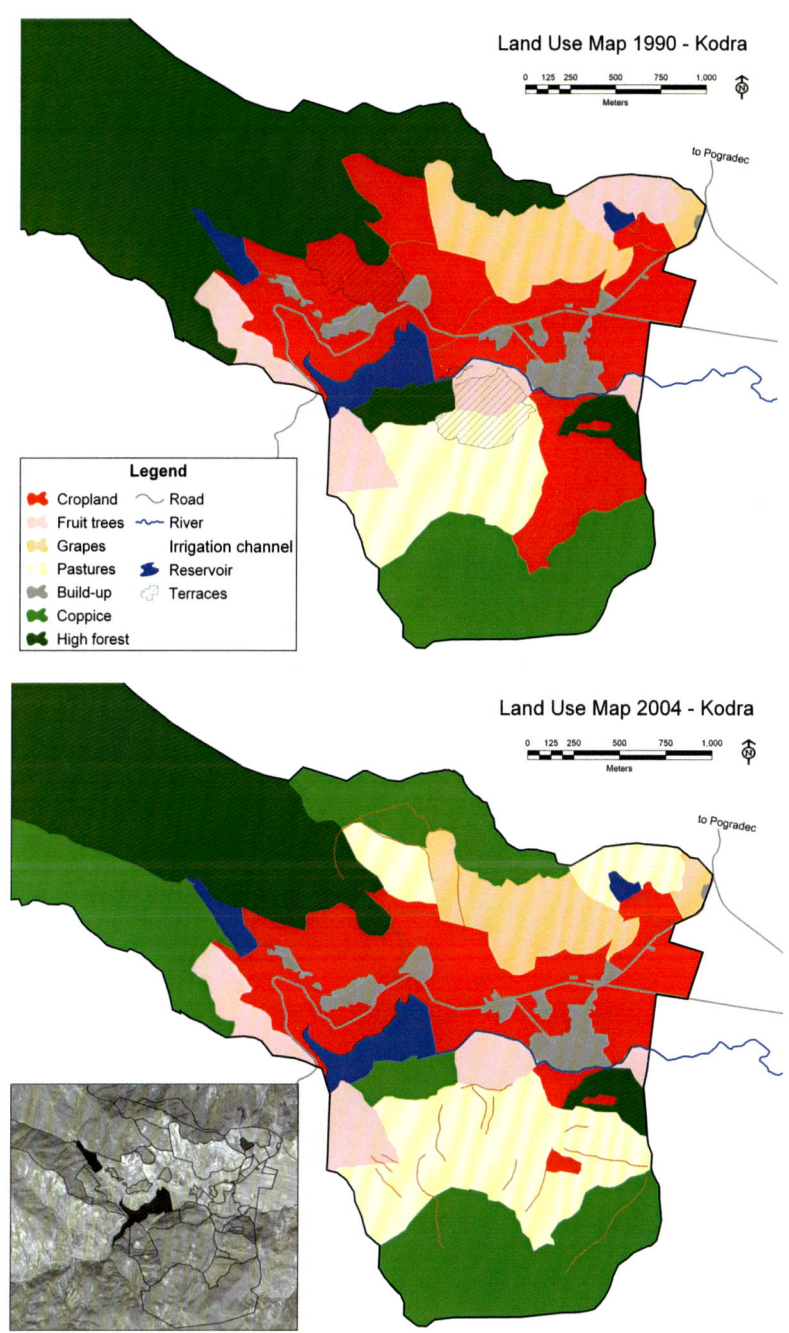

Source: Fieldwork. Maps prepared by Daniel Müller.

Maps 3.3 and 3.4. Land Use in Bagëtia, 1990 and 2004.

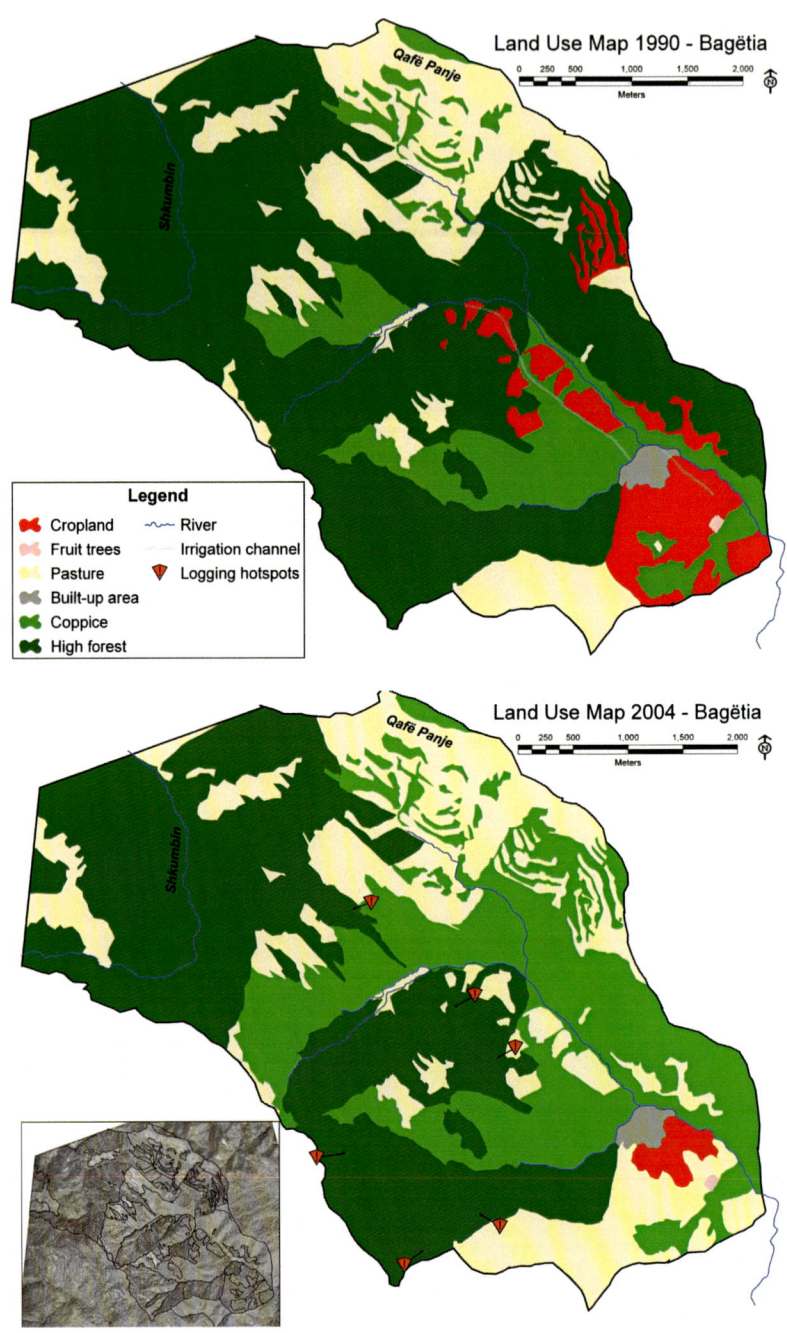

Source: Fieldwork. Maps prepared by Daniel Müller.

PATTERNS OF LAND USE CHANGE 45

Maps 3.5 and 3.6. Land Use in Dardha, 1990 and 2004.

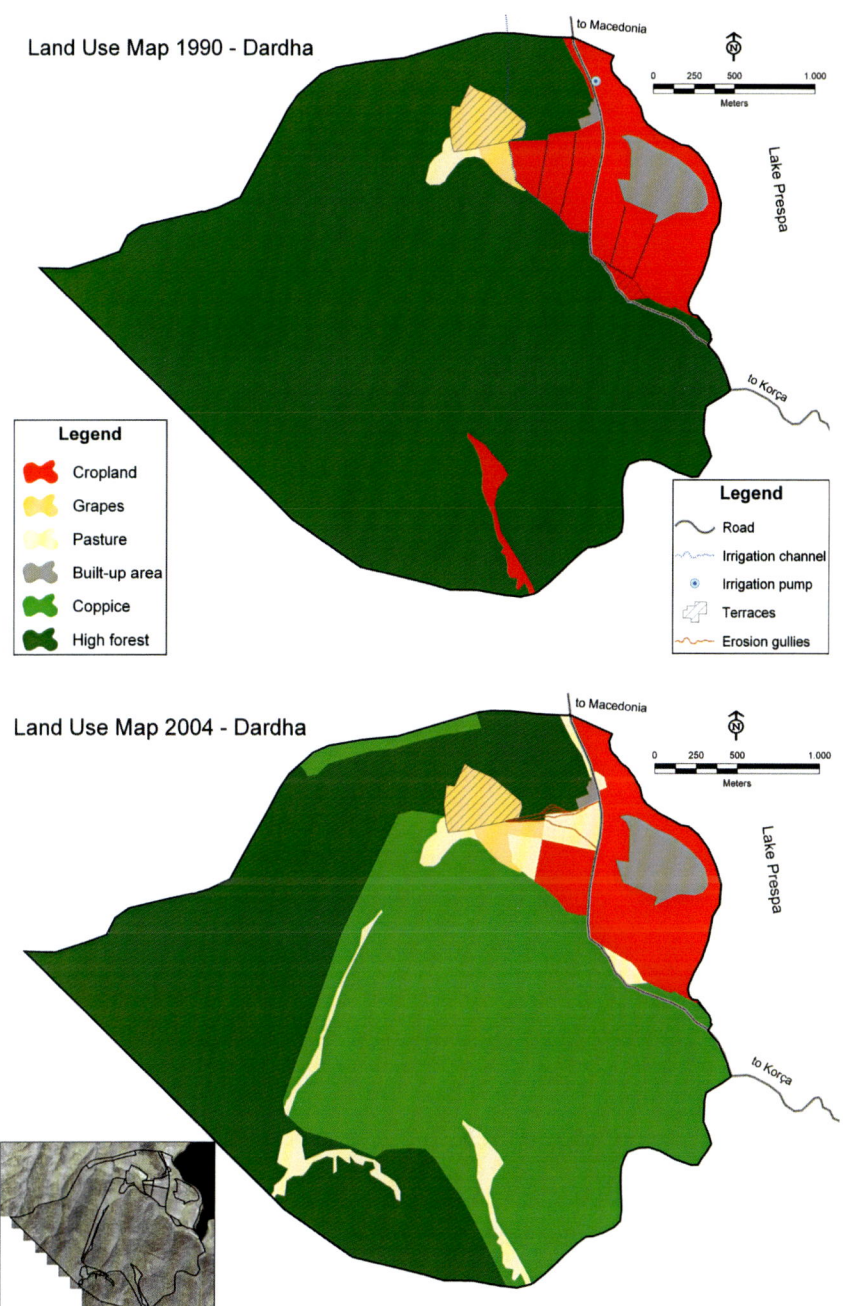

Source: Fieldwork. Maps prepared by Daniel Müller.

Chapter 4

UNMAKING SOCIALIST AGRICULTURE: THE DISSOLUTION OF COLLECTIVE STRUCTURES

The first pattern of land use change I want to examine is the fragmentation of land use as it is reflected in the dissolution of collective structures since the collapse of socialism. I begin with an analysis of the fragmentation of the collective plot structure (and the lack of subsequent land consolidation), and continue with an analysis of the dissolution of irrigation, land terracing, and waste disposal systems in the focus of collective action. Through the analyses I move from the *description* of the pattern of land fragmentation in the previous chapter to its *explanation* through a lens of rent.

The Fragmentation of the Plot Structure

As I have shown in Chapter 3, the collective plot structures in Kodra, Bagëtia and Dardha have undergone extreme fragmentation since the collapse of socialism. The origins of this fragmentation lie in Albania's postsocialist land reform and its peculiar local implementations.

The Postsocialist Land Reform

In 1991, 24 years after the collectivization of agricultural land under socialism, Albania instituted a land reform that sought to re-create private property rights to land. The reform differed substantially from the land reforms in other postsocialist countries (Cungu and Swinnen 1999). Unlike elsewhere in Central and Eastern Europe, Albania's 1991 Law "Concerning the Land" (Land Law) took into account "neither former ownership, nor the land boundaries and sizes before collectivization" (Article 8).[1] In other words, the Law did not restitute land to its former, pre-collectivization owners. Instead, it stipulated the full distribution of all collectivized land on a per capita basis (*për frymë*) to the members of former agricultural cooperatives (Article 5). In addition to cooperative workers, other rural dwellers who were not members of the cooperatives such as state farm employees, teachers, or military personal were awarded land, albeit in smaller quantities (Article 6).

Overall, some 383,000 families received on a per capita basis approximately 500,000 hectares of land through the application of the Land Law (Lusho and Papa 1998, 4). In 2004, 440,000 smallholder families operated on approximately 1.8 million parcels. The average farm was fragmented into three to five parcels with totals 1.5 hectares (Ministry of Agriculture and Food 2002).

Albania may have decided for distribution instead of restitution because full restitution would have recreated the disparate ownership structure prior to collectivization that I have described in Chapter 2. When the Land Law was passed in 1991, there were three main interest groups to be considered: rural managers and socialist elites, pre-collectivization landowners, and rural dwellers that had owned none or very little land prior to collectivization (Cungu and Swinnen 1999). Each of the three groups preferred a distinct policy option. The first, rural managers and socialist elites, favored only minimal reforms such as a basic restructuring of the cooperatives and limited privatization of its assets. The second, pre-collectivization landowners, preferred the "historical justice" option and argued for the full restitution of property rights to former owners. The third and largest of the three groups, rural families without a history of landownership, wanted a "social equity" option and opted for the equal distribution of assets to former cooperative members. To gain the support of the largest part of the rural constituency, policymakers passed the social equity option. The critics of this decision quickly labeled the Land Law a "communist law," as it smacked of the egalitarianism that had been so dominant under socialism.

Local Implementations

To implement its stipulations, the Land Law ordered the establishment of *land commissions* at the national, district and village levels (Article 7). Because it did not contain any details about how to carry out the land distribution, the land commissions, especially at the village level, had considerable discretion in implementing the Law. Unsurprisingly, therefore, local implementations often differed substantially from place to place and from the original legal stipulations. The implementations in Kodra, Dardha and Bagëtia were no exceptions in this regard.

Distribution in Kodra

The land commission in Kodra (*komisioni i fshatit*) consisted of representatives from each of the village's seven quarters (*lagje*) and an agronomist from the cadastral office in Pogradec. The commission worked from August 1991 to June 1992. It generated a population list, which encompassed 1010 people and formed the basis for the per capita distribution, from the commune census on 30 July 1991. Based on this list, the commission distributed 160 of the 240 hectares the cooperative held in Kodra. Of these 160 hectares, 50 were irrigated cropland, 70 were non-irrigated cropland, and about 40 were vineyards. The 80 hectares which were not distributed consisted of the cemetery, the water reservoirs, patches of heavily eroded land, and common grazing land.

With the help of the agronomist, the commission members allocated plots to private households. The commission members agreed that plots, which were already privately used, should not be reallocated. These plots included small homegardens of about 0.15 hectares per household to which villagers had use rights during the cooperative times. They also included another 0.15 hectares per household, which were distributed in 1989 and 1990 in the regime's last, desperate attempt to appease the increasingly discontent, rural workforce.

One of the major concerns of the land commission was ensuring that people received land close to their homes. The commission, therefore, decided to allocate large areas of land to the village quarters first. In a second step, it distributed these areas to the households in the respective quarters. To ensure a fair and equitable distribution, the commission made sure that every household got land of similar quality. In a lottery process, the commission allocated to each household a share of the irrigated, fertile cropland on the valley floor, a piece of the collective vineyard, a plot with fruit trees, and a plot of cropland on the valley slopes. The cropland at the bottom of the valley was divided into two categories of different land quality. Households were given either 450 square meters per capita of the first, or 580 square meters per capita of the second category. Of the non-irrigated cropland on the valley's slopes, each household received 700 square meters per capita. In addition, households were awarded 350 square meters per capita in vineyards and 70 square meters per capita in fruit trees.

The result of the distribution in Kodra was a pronounced fragmentation of land ownership. On average, households received 0.16 hectares per household member distributed over 4.9 plots. The average plot was a mere 0.13 hectares. Land fragmentation in Kodra was thus more pronounced than in the average across Albanian villages (cf. Lusho and Papa 1998).

Distribution in Dardha

As in Kodra, the village commission in Dardha decided on a procedure to delineate the borders between households' new agricultural plots. The commission consisted of villagers elected by the community. The commission chose the former chief of the agricultural sector of the cooperative as its head.

In the months following the declaration of the Land Law, it met with members of the village council (*pleqësi*) and other villagers almost every evening in order to discuss the land distribution process.

As in Kodra, Dardha's households had use rights to 0.15 hectares of land for a homegarden and an additional 0.15 hectares of land distributed in 1989 and 1990. Like in Kodra, the land commission in Dardha agreed that this land should not be reallocated. The commission decided to distribute the remaining agricultural land according to broad categories based on biophysical characteristics such as soil fertility, irrigation status, and slope. To this end, the commission set up three categories. Of the first, most productive category – east of the main road towards the lakeshore – households were awarded 200 square meters per capita. Of the second, less productive category – west of the main road towards the grapes – each household got 700 square meters per capita. Of the third category – grapes – households received 320 square meters per capita.

One of the most debated issues within the commission was whether households should receive all the land of one category in a single place (each household would obtain three relatively large parcels) or whether they should receive land of each category in each of the large cooperative parcels, thus ending up with a much more fragmented and diversified plot structure.

At the time, the vast majority of villagers preferred the second option. The logic of this preference was simple: people were afraid to end up with a single, large, unproductive plot of one category while others with more luck or agricultural expertise received a single, large, productive plot. Fragmentation was a way to make sure that all households ended up with the same standard. This was an important argument both for those who still believed in the doctrines of the communist party and for all those who feared that dishonest commission members were going to distribute plots in the most productive parcels to themselves and leave parcels of lesser quality (and thus lower land rents) to others. After all, the reasoning went, as former agronomists, some of the commission members had more expertise about soil quality than an average villager and could easily manipulate the outcome.

In short, to most villagers the alternatives to fragmentation did not seem safe. One alternative included distributing large, single plots randomly through a lottery system. However, counting on good luck seemed to be just as risky as trusting the members of the distribution commission. Another, more elaborated proposition suggested that each quarter (*lagja*) or clan (*fis*) should get a parcel of a certain category in which individual household plots would be fixed randomly. Again, the idea was dropped because of mutual distrust.

After considering the villagers' strong opinions on the issue, the land commission finally decided that each household was to receive one plot of each category in each of the large cooperative parcels. Once this principle was established, the commission immediately set about to implement the decision.

However, the practicalities of distributing the plots on the actual field sites proved to be challenging. The commission's solution was quite ingenious: it established the length of each cooperative parcel as a fixed value and made the width into a variable which depended on the eligible capita of the household that was going to receive the plot. For example, when the commission distributed *Maliver*, the cooperative's most fertile parcel in Dardha, all villagers were present. Starting from the side of the village, the commission first measured the length of a strip in the semi-circle and then drew the name of the household to whom it was to be allocated from a hat. The width of the strip then depended on the size of the household. Thus, the plots of large households were broader than those of small households (see Photo 4.1).

In sum, land distribution in Dardha led to a highly fragmented pattern of land ownership, just as in Kodra. The land commission distributed 5.7 plots with a total area of 92 hectares to 79 households. Today villagers refer to the fragmented plot structure as "one [plot] from the mother-in-law, one from the mule" (*Një nga krushka, një nga mushka*).[2]

Photo 4.1. Maliver: Long and narrow strips of land distributed to households in Dardha.

Source: IKONOS-Image 09-21-2003.

Restitution in Bagëtia

Unlike Kodra and Dardha, Bagëtia did not implement the land reform according to the stipulations of the Land Law. The village was one of many rural Albanian villages whose inhabitants decided to ignore the national legislation and instead restitute ownership rights to cooperative farmland to its historical owners and their heirs. Severin Kodderitzsch (1999, 33) estimates that about 15 to 20 percent of Albania's agricultural land was restituted on such an ad hoc, unplanned basis.[3]

The decision to ignore the national legislation in Bagëtia, however, was not taken without controversy. Before the village finally agreed upon the method of restitution, three land commissions had attempted to distribute the cooperative land. The first commission was established under the communist regime to distribute 0.15 hectares of cooperative farmland to each household. It worked for less than a week before the order came to dissolve the cooperative. The subsequent commissions did not acknowledge the first commission's distribution. The second land commission intended to implement the legal stipulations of the Land Law. Headed by the former chief of the cooperative, this commission distributed 0.13 hectares per capita. (The figure was chosen because households with this amount of land or less were eligible for social assistance.) Yet, before the second commission was able to issue the provisional land certificates (*tapitë*), the head of the commission left Bagëtia for Greece. It was, therefore, left to a third commission to issue the land certificates. In total, the third commission issued certificates to 70 households for a total of 46 hectares. In 2004 these provisional certificates were still the only *legally* valid form of land ownership in Bagëtia because the cadastral service never conferred formal land titles to villagers.

The distribution mandated by the land commissions, however, was not accepted for long. Families with few members and claims to large areas of ancestral land resisted the distribution. Despite initial pressure by the state and fellow villagers, they restituted ancestral land by force. Maks Dulellari played a crucial role in advocating for and enforcing restitution and resisting equitable distribution on the grounds of historical justice. Maks had worked his father's land for 12 years as a young man until it was collectivized by force. He fought hard to get his land claims recognized by his fellow villagers. The size of Maks' ancestral land was about 10 hectares; it covered several plots the land commissions had assigned to other families in the village. To make his claim on this land clear, Maks planted two and a half hectares of wheat with his wife, children, and grandchildren. Furthermore, he told his fellow villagers:

> "When the cooperative came, you stole my land, my father's land and my grandfather's land. Now I take it back! […] And if someone dares to plant something on it I will kill him!"

To back up his words, Maks always carried an old German carbine. Facing these actions and proclamations, the proponents of distribution called upon the police. According to his account, Maks was arrested and jailed 12 times. The police confiscated his rifle and his family's television set, radio and carpets. Maks remembers, one of the policemen threatening him in jail: "Return the land, or I will crash this chair on your back!" But the pressure and threats did not work. Before Maks' resistance could crumble, other families in the village, who also had claims to ancestral land, began to follow Maks' example and favor restitution as well.

The move from distribution to restitution implied a massive change in the distribution of agricultural land in Bagëtia. Maks and the other proponents of restitution got their way because many of the households simply did not bother to put up a fight. Some of them tried to resist restitution initially but ultimately shied away from the social conflicts their resistance would create with local, powerful men like Maks Dulellari. Moreover, as I will explain in the following chapter, Bagëtia has experienced massive out-migration that eased many of the potential conflicts beginning in 1991. One household, for example, sold its house and left to live in a lowland village after its 0.15 hectare homegarden was

Photo 4.2. Discrepancy between distributed land titles and actual land use in Bagëtia.

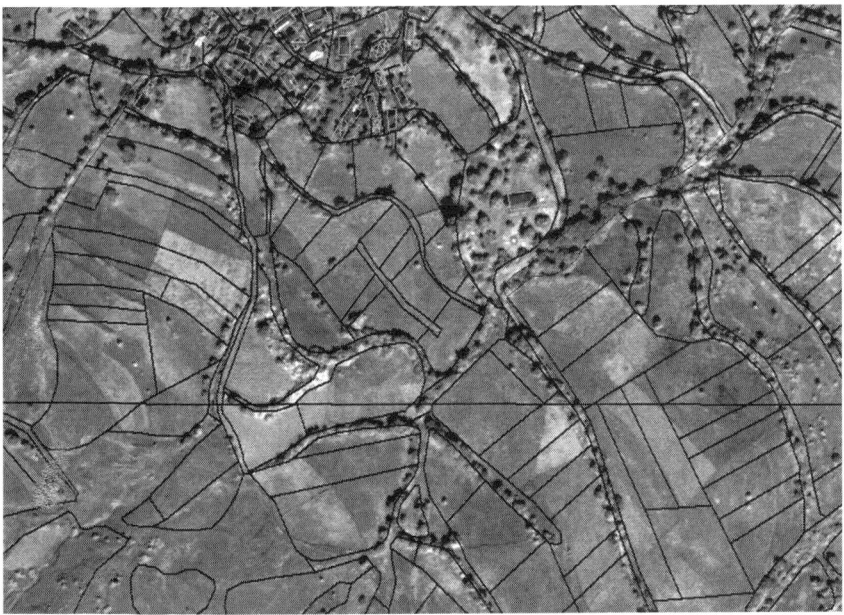

Sources: QuickBird™-Image 08-25-2004 and cadastral map.

Table 4.1. Land fragmentation in the three villages.

	Kodra	Bagëtia	Dardha
1991:			
Total agricultural surface (ha)	160	162	92
Number of households	312	70	79
Type of land reform	distribution	restitution	distribution
Average number of plots given to households	4.9	–	5.7
2004:			
Average number of plots in use per household	3.8	2.6	4.4
Average plot size (ha)	0.13	0.19	0.13
Average area in use per household (ha)	0.5	0.5	0.6
Largest farm size (ha)	1.4	1.3	1.1
Smallest farm size (ha)	0.2	0.1	0.1

Source: Expert Estimations and Household Interviews.

restituted to the pre-collectivization owner. Since the family wanted to leave Bagëtia anyway, they did not bother to put up a fight. The people of Bagëtia, therefore, eventually settled on restituting the land, even though it caused some households (whose ancestors had sold their holdings prior to collectivization) to end up with very little or no land.

As a result of land restitution, de facto land use patterns in 2004 differed markedly from ownership as it was legally registered. Photo 4.2, which shows an overlay of a QuickBird™ satellite image from August 2004 with part of the geo-referenced cadastral map for Bagëtia, illustrates this discrepancy. Very clearly the plots marked on the cadastral map (based on distribution) do not correspond with actual (restituted) plot boundaries.

In sum, the implementation of the land reform in Kodra, Dardha and Bagëtia shows the considerable amount of leeway exercised by villages compared to the legal stipulations of the 1991 Land Law. Yet despite this leeway, together the national legislation and its particular local implementations have facilitated the same result: a sharp fragmentation of plot structures. This fragmentation is summarized in Table 4.1.

Impediments to Land Consolidation

To understand the causes of the fragmentation of land use it is not enough to understand merely why plot structures became fragmented in 1991. It is also important to explain why farmers did not consolidate their fields afterward. I suggest that the answer lies in the particular rent dynamics emerging from the political and economic conditions of postsocialist Albania.

Rent-Seeking in Albanian Politics

Throughout much of the postsocialist period, Albania suffered from political uncertainty and economic instability that severely impeded successful land consolidation. Personal feuds, constant maneuvering, use of violence, and widespread corruption characterized national politics (Pettifer and Vickers 2007, Saltmarshe 2000). While the conventional economy was in shambles, the twilight economy gained increasing importance. Albania became an important transit center for people, arms and drugs trafficked into Western Europe and the Balkans. The country's political parties and bureaucracy were deeply immersed in these activities and provided protection to Mafia-style entrepreneurs for politicians' and bureaucrats' share of the economic rent (Pettifer and Vickers 2007, Saltmarshe 2001). The political and economic crisis climaxed in 1997 in anarchy and a near civil war in which about 2,000 people were killed (Jarvis 2000).

The immediate cause of the 1997 crisis had been the crash of pyramid investment schemes, which dominated Albania's financial system since the collapse of socialism. Approximately two thirds of the population had invested in them. The pyramid schemes had used the deposits of new investors to cover interest payments to the existing investors. Competition for new investors had led to interest rates of up to 15 percent per *month* (with a minimum deposit of 50,000 Lek, 500 DM, or 500 US$) (Voell 2003). The extraordinary returns had proven to be highly attractive to Albanians, although the exact workings of the pyramids had remained unknown to most people. Yet prominent government officials had generated a sense of investment security by endorsing pyramid companies. The government had also ignored the International Monetary Fund's crash warnings in October 1996. The inevitable crash came in January 1997, when no new investors were left to be recruited. The crash wiped out 60 percent of Albania's private savings. According to the World Bank, the capital lost amounted to 1.2 billion US$, about half of Albania's GDP in 1996 (Olson 2000).

The financial collapse led to the widespread breakdown of public order. Thousands of bankrupt investors took to the streets in demonstrations against the kleptocratic elite of pyramid operations and their political backers who were said to have charged rents in exchange for political protection. Popular anger soon escalated into serious riots. From March to July 1997, Albania descended into anarchy. The government was forced to resign, many members of the military and police deserted, and, for the second time after 1991, ordinary Albanians went on a rampage to ransack banks, town halls, courthouses, land registries, police stations and military barracks. The anarchy came to a head when the masses looted military depots and carried off some 600,000 Kalashnikovs (Biberaj 1998). The crisis ended in the summer of 1997 when a newly established interim government took control and, aided by an international intervention force, managed to slowly restore order and stability (Pettifer and Vickers 2007).

Although countrywide turmoil did not occur after 1997, instances of anarchy were still common on the regional level. For example, much of Northern Albania, especially the district of Tropoja, was completely beyond government control for the better part of the late 1990s (Pettifer and Vickers 2007). At the same time, Albanian politics continued to be plagued by widespread corruption, nepotism and illicit rent-seeking. For these reasons, popular resentment of the state reached proverbial dimensions. The oft-heard cry "There is no state, there is no law!" (*s'ka shteti, s'ka ligji!*) accurately sums up people's perceptions of the state.

The political crisis had severe implications for land consolidation. Throughout the postsocialist years, Albanian politics regarding land consolidation were at a standstill. Originally, the architects of the land reform had decided on land distribution based on social equity considerations. Over the course of the 1990s, however, the unresolved issue of historical justice was lingering on. Pushed by international donors, Albania started several initiatives to compensate pre-collectivization landowners. Yet, all of these initiatives were deadlocked by political strategizing. The most recent of the initiatives, the 2004 Law "On Restitution and Compensation of Property" (Compensation Law) passed with considerable delay and, at the time of writing, still awaits implementation.[4] Like other initiatives of its kind, the debates around the Compensation Law were a prodigious field for political rent-seeking. In exchange for votes from their respective constituencies, influential politicians kept the distribution versus restitution debate in a purposeful limbo. At the local level, the uncertainty about whether distribution may be overturned by restitution caused social conflict, tenure insecurity, and dampening investment in land – all factors impeding successful land consolidation (Lemel 1998, 1999, 2000).

Local Conflicts over Rent Distribution

At the local level, the land reform remained a highly controversial topic even after the implementation of the Land Law. When I was talking to people in Kodra, Bagëtia and Dardha, nearly everyone had a distinct opinion on whether distribution or restitution would have been the better policy. The topic remained highly controversial, as the following conversation, overheard in a shared taxi near Kodra, illustrates:

Passenger: "I'm for the return of the property that my father has left me and which belongs to me."

Driver: "But it has already been divided by the state."
P [*insists*]: "It belongs to me because it's mine."
D: "What belongs to you? [*Turning to the other passengers:*] Hey, to whom belongs the land, to him or to God? [*To the first passenger again:*] The land belongs to God and He made it for Man, so it belongs to everybody."
P: "My father has bought it a long time ago, and the others take my land, huh?"
D [*loud*]: "The state has already divided it, and if it's returned to the ex-owners, a civil war will break out and Sali and Fatos will be declared 'Enemies of the People.'"

The conservation reached a critical point here. Sali Berisha was the opposition leader and Fatos Nano was the prime minister at the time this conversation took place. Calling them "enemies of the people" – the term used for those condemned by the socialist regime – was the most dramatic image the driver could invoke to depict the social upheavals that could result from a policy change to restitution. Yet the driver's fervor did not deter the passenger from insisting on his point.

P [*louder*]: "They are assfuckers! If the state wants, it takes your land, and there is nothing you can do!"
D [*conciliatory*]: "The state eats my shit, that's all it does! [But] what you want is that 10 persons eat and 900 others die. No, no, look [*the taxi passes by a cemetery*], two meters belong to us, nothing more."

There are several reasons why the mode of the land reform was debated so controversially more than thirteen years after the passage of the 1991 Land Law. First, land privatization had distributed control over legal access to land and, therefore, largely determined rural people's ability to create land rents. Second, distribution had been a process laden with (illicit) rent-seeking by local elites. And third, many of the accidental errors and technical mistakes made during the implementation caused conflicts among neighbors and fellow villagers. To many people, therefore, it seemed that restitution would have been less arbitrary to implement.[5]

The theme of powerful actors with access to authority runs through the stories of land conflicts like thread. The following examples illustrate: (a) (distrust of) commission member manipulation, (b) use of power by non-commission members to manipulate outcomes, and (c) use of power by neighbors to control access.

Rent-seeking by members of the land commissions and unintentional errors in the distribution process led to serious conflicts among land users. Some of the conflicts occurred immediately after the land commissions had finished their work. Often, members of the land commissions were said to have distributed more or better quality land to themselves than to other villagers. The commission members' claims to land were therefore often the first to be disputed. For example, our host in Dardha, Agron Andoni, had been a member of the village land commission in 1991. An agronomist by training, Agron felt obliged to bring in his expertise in the distribution of the cooperative farmland. He joined the land commission despite the warnings of his wife, Plaguna, who argued that he could only make himself enemies in this position. Plaguna was proven right by the developments after the commission's work was finished: one night in 1992, villagers who believed that Agron had cheated them and distributed more than his share to himself, went out and cut down Agron's grapevines. That same night, they also destroyed the grape plots of two other commission members. Agron told me that over the years he discovered who razed his plot, but he and the others decided to bury the hatchet.

The case of Agron and Plaguna shows that the contestations over land distribution were not just theoretical debates: some villagers used power to manipulate the outcomes after the distribution. Those who did were often powerful, local men – not necessarily land commission members – who used their influence to gain access to land. For another example, Hassan and Mira Proni from Kodra were involved in a dispute about an agricultural parcel for many years. In the course of distribution, the elderly couple received a plot of fertile cropland adjacent to their home. They even received a provisional certificate to the land from the land commission. Yet neither the land commission's decision nor the certificate prevented Bujar Sherifi, a fellow villager and former head of the commune council, from claiming the plot for his own household. Bujar based his claims to the plot on historical rights he held and threatened to destroy any crops planted by the Pronis. The couple responded by filing several futile complaints with the commune administration and Pogradec's deputy to the national parliament. They did not take the issue to court because they believed that Bujar, a powerful man with good connections and influence in regional politics, would have bought the court decision. The Proni's hopes for justice now rest with a Tirana-based anti-corruption non-governmental organization to whom they turned over their case in late 2005.

The last example concerns one of the many conflicts in rural Albania that revolve around road access. In Kodra, I met Dashi Qemali and his wife Luljeta, newcomers to the village, who had bought a house there in the mid-1990s. Dashi and Luljeta's compound was accessible by two public roads: a larger one in the front and a smaller one in the back. Unfortunately for the couple, their backdoor neighbors prohibited them from using the smaller of the two roads, arguing that the Qemalis' cows would pollute the road with their dung. To reach the cowshed in the back of their compound, Dashi and Luljeta, therefore, had to walk their cows through the front lawn alongside their veranda. The two had tried to negotiate with their neighbors, pointing to the fact that the former owner of the house had always used the small road to let his cattle into the compound. Their neighbors, however, stonewalled them. All of the five neighboring households were close relatives, and the Qemalis were newcomers without family in Kodra. In response, Dashi asked the village and commune councils to mediate the conflict, but his efforts were futile. The head of the neighboring clan had been chief of the commune council for many years and was still powerful enough to disrupt any attempts to resolve the conflict.

Taken together, one can understand the conflicts of the Andoni, Proni and Qemali families as conflicts over access to land. The rents that actors derive from control over that access were at stake in each of the conflicts. The rent-seeking of local elites who bypass the legal stipulations of the land reform and other legislation can only be understood as part of the broader dynamics that characterize the postsocialist Albanian state. Rent-seeking at the local level thus mirrored the rent-seeking by national elites described in the previous section. At both levels, rent-seeking was made possible by the general political crisis and the instability of the postsocialist period. It impeded land consolidation and caused land use to remain fragmented.

Rent Creation in Subsistence Farming

Finally, an economic explanation may explain why land users did not consolidate their fields after the initial fragmentation. I suggest that in the absence of the ability to create rents through large-scale farming, many villagers preferred to maintain a diversified set of plots in order to spread risk and cover their own subsistence needs.

Since the collapse of socialism, the conditions for agriculture in Albania have dramatically declined. The decline is closely linked to trade liberalization, which has caused a reduction of subsidies and measures to protect the agricultural sector since 1991. In the wake of trade liberalization, postsocialist governments reduced tariffs on food imports and abolished import permits and quotas. The liberalization was accompanied by a growing agricultural trade deficit. Food imports rose by over 300 percent, while exports of agricultural products fell by more than 76 percent.[6] Contrary to initial expectations, trade concessions by the European Union, Albania's primary trading partner, did not boost agricultural exports.[7] On the contrary, trade liberalization forced Albanian products on the *domestic* market to compete against highly subsidized EU products, mainly from Greece and Italy.

As result of the open borders for agricultural products, Albanian markets became "inundated by imports" (Abdul-Hamid 2003, 8). On the wholesale market in Tirana, for example, foreign agricultural products were regularly 30 to 50 percent cheaper than domestic products. While Albanian farmers encountered difficulties in accessing the necessary machinery, obtaining agricultural credit, receiving extension advice, and purchasing inputs, their EU competitors received yearly subsidies of, on average, 7,000 Euro (Paasch 2003).

Together, these constraints severely restricted the Albanian farmers' ability to create rents through large-scale farming. For this reason, very few attempted to increase land holdings and consolidate their fragmented plot structure. Instead, many withdrew from commercial agriculture and turned to subsistence production. For subsistence production, however, a diversified and fragmented plot structure is often more suitable to farmers' needs than a non-diversified, consolidated plot structure.

In Kodra, Bagëtia and Dardha, for instance, people found ways to mediate the negative aspects of land fragmentation and integrated its advantages into their agricultural strategies. For example, one negative aspect generally associated with land fragmentation is that rents decrease as distance to parcels increases (von Thünen 1966). In this line of reasoning, King and Burton (1982, 471) argue that: "[Land] fragmentation is regarded as a disadvantage because of the waste of time and effort that it entails for moving labour, animals, machinery and harvested crops, and the difficulties of supervision, access, use of irrigation water,

Photo 4.3. Distances of a randomly selected household to its plots in Dardha.

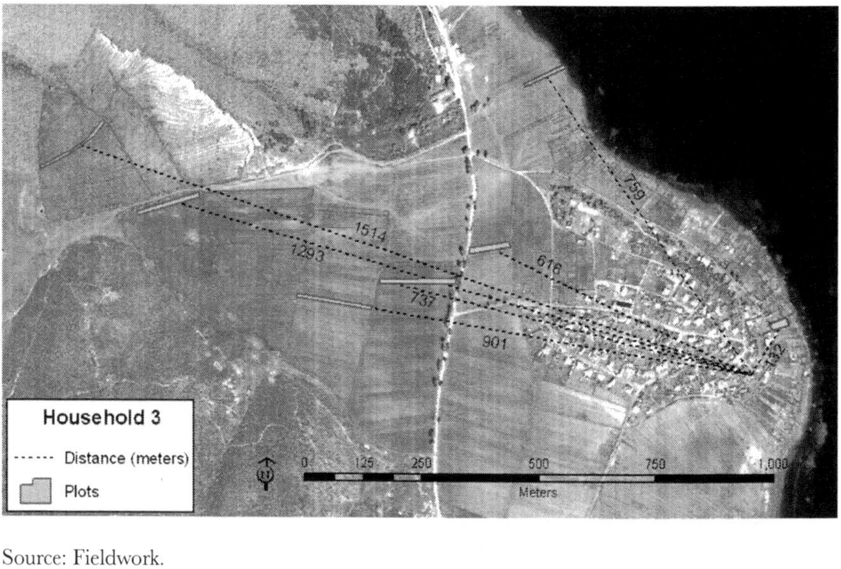

Source: Fieldwork.

disease control etc." To the farmers in Kodra, Bagëtia and Dardha, however, the distance argument was of little relevance. Generally, the distances from their homes to their plots were short. In Dardha, for instance, the average distance from a farming household to its plots was only 700 meters. Photo 4.3 shows a randomly selected household and the exact distances to each of its plots. In this example, the household's most distant plot was just 1.5 kilometers away (as the crow flies). This amounted to about a 25 minute trip, which was not an unreasonable commuting time, especially considering that the opportunity costs of labor were low for most farmers in Dardha. Furthermore, the farmer might have visited two or more plots on a single trip and, thus, save time.

Another disadvantage generally associated with land fragmentation is the small size and often irregular shape of fields. The rationale is that operating large machinery on small, irregular fields is difficult, and moving machinery from one field to the next is costly and causes delays as the heavy equipment is dismantled and reassembled. Yet, in many Albanian villages, farmers have developed strategies to overcome these constraints. In Kodra, for example, 70 percent of the cropland was plowed with horses. Farmers were able substitute horses for tractors and, thereby, dodge monopolistic tractor operators who extracted high rents in return for their services. In Dardha, on the other hand, villagers cooperated in the management of their wheat and corn fields. Together they hired two or three tractors at the beginning of each planting season. Just as in the cooperative, the tractors plowed entire parcels containing up to 50 individual plots. During the harvesting season, this pattern was repeated with jointly contracted combine harvesters.

Thus, many farmers in rural Albania have been able to mitigate some of the important disadvantages associated with land fragmentation. Moreover, they have also successfully incorporated many of its advantages into their production strategies. One of the most important advantages is that a fragmented plot structure allows farmers to spread risk. For example, even in the relatively homogenous environments of Kodra, Bagëtia and Dardha there are subtle microclimatic differences in soil type, insolation, moisture, wind and so forth. Hail, plant disease, and insect pests could strike in one field and leave others untouched. Having a number of non-adjacent plots thus spread farmers' risk of crop failure.

Another advantage of land fragmentation is that it allowed farmers to use multiple eco-zones. A mix of meadows and pastures, subsistence gardens, vineyards, grain fields and forest was of vital importance as a safety net that provided for the basic subsistence needs. As Vasil Meksi, a subsistence farmer from Bagëtia, put it: "The land gives it all! [...] We are lucky we have the mountains here, because otherwise we would have died. We have them for livestock, for wood, for everything!"

Critics of land fragmentation in Albania often overlook the advantages of land fragmentation for farmers' food security.[8] Focusing on fragmentation as an impediment to commercial agriculture, they fail to grasp the importance of access to land to cover the most basic subsistence needs of the larger section of the rural population.

The findings from Kodra, Bagëtia and Dardha suggest an economic explanation for the lack of plot structure consolidation after the initial fragmentation. In the absence of the ability to create rents through large-scale farming, the majority of land users turned to subsistence-based agricultural strategies in which a fragmented plot structure is a vital ingredient.

In sum, based on the evidence presented so far, I suggest that plot structures in Albania remained fragmented for broader political and economic reasons. First, the political crisis and instability of the postsocialist period facilitated illicit rent-seeking by elites at the national and local level which impeded successful land consolidation. At the same time, farmers' inability to create rents through large-scale farming facilitated a move towards subsistence agriculture in which a mixed portfolio of plots was essential to spread risk and use land as a safety net.

Changes in Collective Action

In addition to the fragmentation of plot structures, there were other indications of the fragmentation of land use, including the breakdown of irrigation systems, the deterioration of terraces, and the overload of waste disposal systems. I will now explain the dissolution of these structures by focusing on changes in the rents available to collective action.

During socialism collective action regarding rural land use was centered on providing inputs for agricultural production and generating sufficient outputs to feed the population. Cooperative brigades built and maintained terraces, water reservoirs, irrigation channels and drainage canals. In so-called *aksione* (actions), the regime sent military recruits, students and city dwellers out into the countryside to build rural infrastructure or help in agriculture and forestry. Under the slogan "Let's make the mountains and hills as fertile as the fields!" *aksionistët* (the people who engaged in *aksione*) built terraces, helped harvest the crops during peak seasons, and converted forests and swamps into arable fields.[9] Under the slogan "Let's make the village like the town!" they built roads, railways, and health centers.[10] Each year the month of December was designated "month of the forest," and young people had to contribute to afforestation projects (Meta 1993).

After the collapse of the socialist regime, these collective arrangements disappeared, and the collective production of inputs and outputs drastically declined. For example, the local water user associations, which had been in charge of the irrigation infrastructure since the mid-1990s, typically lacked the technical, financial, and administrative capacity to keep the socialist irrigation systems functioning without state involvement (Kodderitzsch 1999). The individual landowners now responsible for the upkeep of the terraces were generally overburdened by this task. Similarly, the waste disposal system collapsed in many villages in the postsocialist period. Dardha, for example, had been spotlessly clean during socialism because the villagers had taken trash to a field where it was burned and buried. In theory, the village had a designated spot for households to dump their trash in the postsocialist period. In practice, however, the dump was empty and trash was disposed of randomly all over the village terrain where it polluted roadsides, vegetable gardens, and runoff rainwater.

Despite the dissolution of these forms of collective action, collective action did not cease to exist. Instead, the postsocialist period was characterized by a change in the focus of collective action. Collective efforts began to be focused in new areas, particularly, the marketing of individually produced outputs and the acquisition of capital, knowledge and technology. Two apt examples of this trend are Kodra's farmers' and credit associations.

The main goal of the farmers' association (*shoqatë e fermereve*) was to create rents for its members by creating access to breed-improved livestock and to the grape market. Collective arrangements were an integral component of its work. For example, the association cooperated with Heifer Project International (HPI), an American aid organization that distributes breed-improved livestock races to farmers in developing countries. To receive livestock from HPI, members of the farmers' association were required to pass on the first female offspring to other members. (HPI calls this "passing on the gift"). In a similar collective arrangement, the farmers' association tried to gain market power by pooling the grapes harvested by its members and collectively selling them to *Rilindja*, a privately-owned distillery in Korça. The association had an exclusive 5-year contract with *Rilindja* that specified the amount of grapes to be delivered as well as their variety and sugar content.

Kodra's credit association (*shoqëria kursim-kredi*) is another example of the general shift in collective action away from joint production under socialism. By controlling access to capital, the association focused on the creation of rents and their redistribution among its members. Members could enter up to a maximum of 20 percent of the credit association's capital into its savings account at a bank in Pogradec. The savings account received 3.2 percent annual interest. Of this amount, 2.5 percent was passed on as credit to the association members and 0.7 percent was kept in order to increase the association's savings. Despite the fact that the credit association paid lower interest than a private bank, its members still preferred it because banks not only charged substantial fees for opening and maintaining accounts, but also often did not deal with small savings.

As illustrated in these two examples from Kodra, the initiatives for new types of collective action were often triggered by outsiders. The idea to found Kodra's farmers' association, for example, came from an USAID project working in Pogradec during the 1990s. Similarly, the foundation of the credit association had been stimulated by Land o' Lakes, an American company that offers financial expertise to farmers' associations.

Since the early 1990s, therefore, collective action in marketing and for the acquisition of agricultural inputs had clearly made headway. Collective action in the production process, on the other hand, was often lacking. One exception was in livestock herding where shepherd families pooled their labor power to herd their sheep and goats together. Except for joint herding, other production processes, such as making hay, milking or slaughtering, were done individually. When I asked members of Kodra's farmers' association about joint production (e.g., jointly using technical equipment like irrigation pumps or rotary cultivators), the farmers showed very little interest. Many simply replied: "Nah, we've had too much of that during the cooperative!" The fact that collective action was reminiscent of cooperatives and had become thoroughly discredited among farmers was also pointed out by Bashkim Zela, the leader of the farmers' association. Bashkim quickly corrected my initial translation of the association's full name as "farmers' cooperative" by emphasizing that it was indeed *not* a "cooperative" but an "association."

Taken together, the analysis of the dissolution of large land use structures built under socialism and the analysis of the fragmentation of plot structures reveal similar dynamics. In both cases, broader political and economic forces such as market liberalization and a decline in the state's coercive power caused shifts in the creation and distribution of the rent available to collective action. The shifts affected land users' incentives and changed the collective land use practices that had created and maintained these structures under socialism.

Chapter 5

UNRAVELING THE SOCIALIST COUNTRYSIDE: DIFFERENTIATION AMONG VILLAGES AND ITS EFFECTS ON LAND USE

When I first came to Bagëtia in June 2004, I felt like I was entering a ghost-village. Klodian and I had accompanied two friends from Kodra who were visiting relatives in Kumbull, the village next to Bagëtia. On the way to Bagëtia, we had passed extensive mountain pastures and a few, fenced-off hayfields. Except for one or two shepherds in the distance, we had not seen any people along the way. When we reached Bagëtia, we found the village practically empty. Many of the picturesque, natural stone houses with their slate-shingled roofs lay abandoned in the sun. The village's cultural center (*vatra e kulturës*), which had been built under socialism, was a crumbling ruin. There were no shops or bars in sight. The few children of the village were in school, and the men had taken their sheep and goats to graze on the alpine slopes. Only an occasional old lady carrying a bucket of water home or spinning wool in the shadows of a dilapidated cooperative building reminded us that there were still people living here.

The contrast between Bagëtia and Kodra, where we were living at that time, could not have been any starker. Kodra was a bustling agricultural village in the lowlands where Klodian and I spent most of our time talking to full or part-time farmers. Kodra had a functioning irrigation system, a farmers' and a credit association, a garage to repair cars and agricultural implements, and even a small agricultural pharmacy, where one could buy pesticides and chemical fertilizer. In addition, a mosque, a protestant church, four grocery stores, three bars, a restaurant, a physician's office, and even a private language school stood as a testament to the village's dynamism.

The difference in development between Kodra and Bagëtia was even more striking, considering that the two villages had experienced relatively equal levels of land use and socioeconomic development under socialism. Collectivization, state planning, infrastructure investments and equal treatment of ethnic groups had largely leveled the differences among them. We plainly observed, that less than fifteen years after the fall of socialism Kodra and Bagëtia had become markedly differentiated. In this chapter I trace the dynamics leading to the differentiation among villages. Specifically, by drawing on case studies from Kodra, Bagëtia and Dardha, I examine how and why land use intensity increased in some villages and decreased in others. I also connect land use intensification and extensification to the growing socioeconomic differentiation among villages. In doing so, I explain the causes and mechanisms of the second pattern of land use change identified in Chapter 3: the differentiation of land use among villages.

The Political Ecology of Land Use in Kodra, Bagëtia and Dardha

Intensification of Land Use in Kodra

Unlike many villages in rural Albania, Kodra's population remained stable after the collapse of socialism. In 2004, the village was home to 1,050 inhabitants in 312 households. While just seven families had sold their houses and permanently left the village after 1991, about the same number of newcomers arrived from the more remote villages of the *Gorë* and *Mokra* mountains. Part of what attracted these newcomers to Kodra was the urban amenities and markets of the nearby town of Pogradec. Pogradec was just eight kilometers away and could easily be reached from Kodra within 20 minutes on one of the frequently departing minibuses or shared taxis. Kodra was also conveniently located on the Tirana-Korça road and, thus, had an excellent connection both to the capital and to the central town of southeastern Albania.

By 2004, land use in Kodra had dramatically changed compared to cooperative times. In 1991, after the implementation of the Land Law, farmers in Kodra, just as elsewhere in Albania, were enthusiastic about their newly acquired property rights to land. They immediately set out to put them into practice. They started planting their new private plots with wheat and corn – the same crops they had planted under the cooperative. However, just as in other Albanian villages, the results in Kodra were disappointing.[1] Yields were much lower than during the cooperative because the use of fertilizers had plummeted and irrigation and drainage channels not been maintained. Crop cultivation did not pay because output prices dropped as a result of foreign competition, and input prices soared. The decreasing profitability motivated farmers to alter their cropping strategies and cultivate more capital and labor intensive crops, such as fruits and vegetables (see Chapter 3).

In a second kind of reaction to the constraints faced in agriculture, many villagers from Kodra turned to off-farm activities, such as wage labor in the service sectors of Pogradec and Korça, migration, or self employment in small businesses. Among these activities, migration became particularly prevalent. Some families sent young members to work abroad right after the breakdown of the cooperative. When the agricultural terms of trade deteriorated in the following years, other families followed suit. By 2004, 55 percent of households in Kodra had at least one member working in another country permanently or seasonally.

Greece, Italy and Macedonia were the three primary destinations for migrants from Kodra. Due to its proximity and high wages, Greece became the favored destination. Greece was particularly popular after 1997, when the Greek economy entered a boom period. Between 1997 and 2004, for example, wages in Greece almost doubled. The rise in salaries reflected an increasing demand for labor that Albanian migrants were happy to fill. In the years prior to the Olympic Summer Games in Athens in 2004, the construction industry boomed in preparations for the Games and the demand for labor accelerated further. Italy was the second most popular destination for residents of Kodra, but was more difficult to reach than Greece. Just as in Greece, working in Italy was enticing because wages were high and employment was easier to find than in Albania. Macedonia was a third destination for workers from Kodra. There, work was still easier to find than in Albania but because Macedonia had much lower wage rates than Greece or Italy, it was a last resort for those unable to find work elsewhere.

Despite the demand for workers and availability of good wages, reaching Greece and Italy was difficult for villagers from Kodra. As ethnic Albanians, they faced strong restrictions to migration for years. Despite two Greek regularization programs in 1998 and 2002 – through which more than 300,000 Albanian immigrants were legalized (Fakiolas 2003, Konidaris 2005) – Greek immigration policies remained restrictive toward all Albanians except members of the Vlach and Greek minorities. Only those who already had an employment history in Greece were able to obtain visas, which granted entry for a period of three months. Even with proper visas, migrants were sometimes turned back at the border without justification or had their visas cancelled by Greek police (cf. Nicholson 2002, 2004). Those who did enter Greece faced severe discrimination. As a result of these constraints, many migrants who worked in Greece in the early 1990s later moved to Italy, where conditions were better (King and Vullnetari 2003). But even in Italy, negative attitudes towards Albanians went hand in hand with increasingly restrictive immigration policies. For example, the Bossi-Fini Law of 2002 criminalized undocumented migration and further tightened the rules for expulsion (Carletto et al. 2004, Kelly 2005).

Nevertheless, despite restrictive immigration laws and discrimination, many ethnic Albanians continued to migrate into Greece and or Italy (cf. Nicholson

2002). Many migrants from Kodra, for example, crossed the border to Greece illegally. Most of them already knew their route through the mountains from past experience. Others chose to go with a local smuggler who took people to Greece via Macedonia for 900 Euro per person.[2] After two months of good work, migrants from Kodra calculated, the cost of the trip had paid off.[3] Especially for the young men in Kodra, (illegal) migration was often more attractive than working full- or part-time in agriculture at home. Lumi Sherifi, one of the young migrants, explained it to me in this way:

> "[In Kodra] we still work the land with the plow and donkeys like in the old days [before socialism]. At first sight it may seem that I'm lazy, but before I start working in the field, I carefully calculate whether it's worth it or not. [...] Us young ones like to go to bars to drink something and if you work in agriculture you can't do this because agriculture gives you money once a year. And so the young go to Greece or find a job [in town] to have money in the pocket everyday. Now look, my mom, my dad, and my wife have gone to plant onions. They started 5 days ago, and it needs about 10 more to finish planting. But to hoe and to collect them, they will need about 60 days in total. And if you sell them, they don't bring in more than 40,000 Lek [320 Euro]. With these 40,000 Lek, what can you do first? Eat? The children need books and clothing for school! [...] In Greece, I earn this money in 10 days."

Not all workers or families shared Lumi's perspective on migration; due to the legal restrictions imposed by Greek immigration law, many families from Kodra could not, or would not, send family members abroad. In a third type of reaction to the constraints in agriculture, these families often sought employment in the nearby urban centers of Pogradec or Korça. Yet finding employment was often difficult because the socialist mining industry (the main source of employment outside of agriculture during socialism) had not survived the system change. In response, many of these families opened small-scale businesses, such as little stores or bars. More recently, some have also started processing agricultural products.

The sources of income for residents of Kodra reflect the villagers' constraints and the choices they made between agriculture, migration and off-farm activities. In 2004, agriculture accounted for only 17 percent of overall household income, in comparison to eight percent from remittances and 69 percent from off-farm activities. Sixty percent of households had found work in the construction or service industries in Pogradec and Korça, 23 percent lived mainly on seasonal labor migration or remittances, and 17 percent were full-time farmers or shepherds. Yet, many of those whose principal occupation was outside of agriculture continued farming on a part-time or subsistence basis. These developments meant that villagers had adapted their livelihood strategies and their land use to the changing economic opportunities. Compared to other villages like Bagëtia and Dardha, land use in Kodra remained relatively intensive. The new (part-time) farmers largely stopped producing grain, introduced onions and other vegetables as cash crops, and dramatically raised the productivity of grapes. In the livestock sector, they increased the number of cattle, sheep and goats and raised their productivity by introducing new breeds.

Extensification of Land Use in Bagëtia

When the cooperative broke down, 350 people lived in Bagëtia distributed over 70 households. By 2004, the village population had shrunk to merely 99 inhabitants in 25 households. Deteriorating living conditions contributed to the drastic population decrease. In 2004, the entire village shared only three public faucets. In winter, the village was often cut off electricity for days at a time. The villagers could no longer receive Albanian radio or TV stations – but the satellite dishes dotting their houses allowed them to view Greek, German and Italian channels. If they wanted to make a phone call, they had to walk up-mountain about 500 meters before their cell phones reached the network. Perhaps most importantly, the school building lay in shambles. The school had only five students who were taught together in the one remaining classroom. It offered only grades 1 – 4 (*shkolla fillore*), and students had to attend the elementary school in Kumbull for the remaining grades, 5–8. Walking the rugged mountain path that connects the two villages took one and a half hours in the summer and more than two hours in the winter.[4]

Like the public infrastructure, agricultural production in Bagëtia collapsed after the decollectivization of the cooperative. Compared to Kodra, biophysical conditions (e.g., temperature, slope or soil fertility) in Bagëtia are much less favorable to crop production. Under the new, postsocialist political and economic conditions, the immense old-growth forests and mountain pastures surrounding the village had simply become too high and too steep for viable crop production.

Furthermore, market access was much more constrained in Bagëtia than in Kodra. After the collapse of socialism, the gravel road connecting Bagëtia to the lowland plains of Pogradec and Korça quickly became impassable due to a lack of maintenance. In 2004, catching a minibus from Bagëtia to Maliq, a small market town in the district of Korça, required walking an hour along a narrow mountain path. From there, a bus ran once a day, usually early in the morning. Most supplies were brought into Bagëtia on foot or on mule- or horseback along the mountain path. Only in summer, when the sun had dried the ground from the spring rains, could IFA-trucks reach Bagëtia to bring in more bulky, yearly supplies like flour and construction materials.[5]

In addition to the deteriorating infrastructure and the constraints faced in agriculture, living conditions in Bagëtia were worsened by a complete lack of local employment opportunities. In the early 1990s, families began looking for new livelihood strategies beyond their village. For them, just as for their peers in Kodra, the jobs and living conditions abroad proved to be highly attractive. Yet, in contrast to Kodra, Greek immigration policy eased the migration of villagers from Bagëtia. Greek law facilitated the immigration of people from Bagëtia because of their Vlach identity (cf. Konidaris 2005). In the national Greek view, Hellenic heritage had been passed on through Byzantine culture to today's Greek Orthodox religion. Religion thus classified all Albanian Vlachs (and all other Albanian Greek Orthodox) as of Greek origin (Schwandner-Sievers 1999, 2f).

The ease of access to Greece exerted a tremendous pull on people from Bagëtia. Most of the 45 households that left the village between 1991 and 2004 went to Greece. For a fee of 15 Euro, they were able to obtain 3-year working visas (*viza 3-vjeçare*). If they were registered in Greece, passed a Vlach language test, and were of an appropriate age, they were even entitled to receive a pension of 200 Euro per month from the Greek state (*pensioni i grekut*). Moreover, compared to their ethnic Albanian or Macedonian fellow citizens, the Vlachs who emigrated to Greece integrated more easily into Greek society. They were not subject to the same degree of discrimination that ethnic Albanians or Macedonians faced in Greece.

In Bagëtia, emigration dramatically affected people's livelihood strategies. By 2004, 44 percent of the households in the village lived on seasonal labor migration and remittances sent from abroad; 32 percent received state salaries, social assistance or pensions; and 24 percent derived their main income from livestock production.

Regarding land use, these developments meant that villagers had dramatically de-intensified their agricultural practices. While the cooperative had cultivated even the most remote and unproductive mountain pastures, by 2004 crop production in Bagëtia had virtually ceased. The villagers had turned cropping land into pasture, or, less frequently, cultivated former cropping land with fodder plants. Livestock production, mostly oriented towards subsistence needs, had become villagers' primary agricultural occupation (see Chapter 3).

Extensification of Land Use in Dardha

As in Kodra, the number of people living in Dardha has changed little since the collapse of socialism. By 2004, the village had grown by two households, totaling 340 people in 81 households. Dardha's demographic stability can be attributed largely to the new livelihood strategies the villagers were forced to develop after the breakdown of the cooperative.

As in Bagëtia, the conditions that supported viable commercial agriculture in Dardha rapidly deteriorated after decollectivization. Most importantly, much of the village's irrigation infrastructure was looted in the upheavals of 1991, seriously diminishing the productivity of the once fertile land. By 2004, water scarcity had become a tremendous and ironic problem, since the village is located on the shores of Lake Prespa, one of the largest lakes of Albania. The dysfunctional irrigation system had not been replaced, and the karstic geology of the *Mal i Thatë* Mountains immediately seeped away the rainwater.[6]

Similar to Bagëtia, lack of market access became another major impediment for commercial agriculture in Dardha. Located forty kilometers away from Korça (and just five kilometers from the Macedonian border), it took farmers three hours to reach the nearest Albanian market on a bumpy gravel road in 2004. To make matters worse, they had to rely on public transportation. Although markets in the small Macedonian towns across the border were geographically closer, they remained inaccessible for agricultural produce from Dardha for other reasons. Although Albania and Macedonia had signed a trade agreement which made the Prespa region a free trade zone, all cross border trade in agricultural produce was unidirectional from Macedonia to Albania. Albanian agricultural produce was never sold in Macedonia because it could not compete with Macedonian produce, which was less costly and was often perceived to be of higher quality.[7]

As agriculture was no longer a profitable activity, the villagers of Dardha had to look for alternative livelihood strategies. Over the course of the 1990s, some households opened small businesses in the local service sector or started working for the local administration. Most, however, began to look across the border for new opportunities. Not only was the Macedonian border closer than the next urban center in Albania, but being ethnic Macedonians, the villagers did not face restrictions on migrating to Macedonia and taking up employment there (King and Vullnetari 2003:32). Instead, they received preferential treatment by Macedonia, especially with regard to employment. Macedonia was one of the few countries that allowed visa-free entry to Albanian citizens in general, but regarding labor migration procedures were especially favorable to ethnic Macedonians. Their ethnicity entitled them to unrestricted entry because of the weight the Former Yugoslav Republic of Macedonia accorded to ethnic identity. The Macedonian state defined an ethnic Macedonian (*Makedonec*) as someone who was an Orthodox Christian, spoke Macedonian, and identified himself as Macedonian (Perry 1997). This emphasis on ethnic identity was reflected not only in Macedonia's recent secession from former Yugoslavia in 1991 but also in the culmination of its nation-building process which the country had pursued since the end of World War II (ibid.). For this reason, the constitution of Macedonia specifically mentions a "concern for the status and rights of persons belonging to the Macedonian people in neighboring countries" (Constitution of the Republic of Macedonia, Article 49). Thus, it became common practice for the Macedonian state to grant citizenship to ethnic Macedonians living in Albania. This meant that virtually all of the villagers of Dardha held dual citizenships in 2004.

The jobs available in Macedonia proved highly attractive to the people of Dardha. Over the course of the 1990s, a growing number of households began sending a member or two to Macedonia for seasonal employment. They took on jobs as masons, master bricklayers (*ustallaret*), and hired hands in agriculture. Although wages in Macedonia were not much higher than in Albania, it was much easier to find work there. By 2004, seasonal labor migration to Macedonia had become the most popular way to make a living in Dardha. The migrants usually worked in Macedonia for three to nine months a year and returned home during the winter months. Of the 81 households in the village, 45 had at least one member working seasonally in Macedonia. There were only 24 households that did not engage in any seasonal labor migration, and 12 households had members seasonally working in Greece.[8]

Overall, the constraints faced in agriculture and the subsequent turn to seasonal labor migration meant that by 2004, 70 percent of households in Dardha derived their main income from seasonal labor migration. Thirty percent lived of state salaries or worked in the local tertiary sector. Agricultural production was the main source of income for none of the households.

Regarding land use, these developments brought about a change towards more extensive land use strategies. Yet, despite the decrease in labor availability caused by migration, the villagers abandoned a much smaller area of cropland than their peers in Bagëtia. At the same time, they did not switch to more profitable crops to the same extent as their peers in Kodra, even though virtually all households in Dardha were left intact. Instead, the villagers continued to grow wheat and corn because poor soils and water scarcity inhibited the cultivation of more profitable crops, such as vegetables. Wheat and corn production yielded acceptable results even at very low input levels and provided straw and forage to feed the villagers' livestock in winter (see Chapter 3).

Taken together, the comparison of the political and economic conditions for land use since the collapse of socialism in Kodra, Bagëtia and Dardha indicates significant variation among the three villages. The comparison suggests that land use practices in the three villages were influenced by three main factors: ethnically differentiated migration strategies, market access, and biophysical conditions. I will now use rent as an analytical lens for exploring the reasons why the three factors have gained such importance in the postsocialist period.

Factors Differentiating Land Use among Villages

Ethnicity

Ethnicity has shaped the land use dynamics among villages because it determined the shares of rent villagers were able to capture in foreign labor markets. When countries like Greece, Italy or Macedonia control access to their labor markets via immigration policies that differentiate access along ethnic lines, they create rent which the actors involved in those labor markets may capture. Throughout the 1990s and 2000s, the immigration policies of Albania's neighbors impeded access to foreign labor markets for some ethnic categories and facilitated access for others. Migrants who enjoyed privileged access were able to obtain shares of the rent distributed among the actors in the respective labor market. Migrants who faced restricted access were unable, or at least faced severe difficulties in obtaining such shares. The opportunity to capture rent abroad determined the allocation of household labor between agriculture and emigration, and thereby, shaped the nature of land use and land use change.

Table 5.1 clearly demonstrates the link between emigration and ethnicity. The table shows the percentage of households in Kodra, Bagëtia and Dardha with at least one member permanently or seasonally working abroad. It suggests that ethnicity has been a crucial factor determining the intensification and extensification of land use among villages. For the ethnic Albanians of Kodra, for example, the immigration policies of neighboring countries made migration more difficult than for the Vlachs of Bagëtia and the Macedonians of Dardha. Migration rates in Kodra were therefore significantly lower than in the other two villages. As a result of the impediments to migration, much of the labor in Kodra remained tied to village, where a large number of people continued to depend on agriculture. Out of necessity, these people developed strategies to make intensive use of their land. The Vlachs of Bagëtia, on the other hand, faced virtually no restrictions on working in Greece. The ease of access exerted a tremendous pull on the village population. As villagers left in masses over the course of the 1990, the resulting

Table 5.1. Emigration by ethnicity and destination in 2004.

	Greece	Macedonia	Italy	No Migration
Kodra (Ethnic Albanians)	32%	3%	20%	45%
Bagëtia (Vlachs)	84%	0%	0%	16%
Dardha (Macedonians)	15%	55%	0%	30%

Source: Household interviews (n = 74).

labor shortage facilitated the dramatic extensification of land use in Bagëtia. Finally, the Macedonians of Dardha could freely move between Albania and Macedonia. The absence of legal barriers to migration, coupled with better employment opportunities abroad, had decreased the availability of labor for agriculture and facilitated an extensification of land use.

Market Access

Differences in market access shape land use because they directly translate into the creation of land rent. Johann Heinrich von Thünen, the "father" of the spatial analysis of rent dynamics has argued that land rent is created through differences in market distance and thus transportation costs. It declines with increasing distance from the market, but the rate of decline varies for each crop according to its transportation cost. Therefore, villages further away from the market tend to produce crops that are easier to transport but are of lower value than the crops produced in villages closer to the market. Land use, in other words, tends to de-intensify with increasing distance from markets (Thünen 1966 [1826]).[9]

In Kodra, Bagëtia and Dardha, differential market access created different amounts of land rent available to land users in the three villages. In each village, market access shaped the allocation of household capital and labor between agriculture and off-farm activities in different ways. As a result, the villages with better market access displayed more intensive land use than the villages where market access was restricted.

Table 5.2 summarizes the most salient features regarding market access in the three villages. The table corroborates the theoretical explanation which suggests that access to market outlets and off-farm opportunities was a key influence on land use.

In Kodra, as the table suggests, proximity to the market facilitated agricultural intensification. Households could easily transport agricultural

Table 5.2. Market access.

	Kodra	Bagëtia	Dardha
Distance from market (km)	8	25	40
Road conditions	asphalt road	gravel road	gravel road
Distance to road (min)	5	60	5
Preferred means of transportation	shared taxi	minibus	bus
Frequency (departures/day)	~100	1	2
Traveling time to market (min)	20	180	180

Source: Fieldwork.

produce and inputs to and from the market and, therefore, kept capital and labor in agriculture. Moreover, the very proximity of off-farm opportunities allowed households to engage in both off-farm activities and part-time farming, thus, retaining capital and labor in agriculture that under other circumstances would have been lost to off-farm employment.

In Bagëtia and Dardha, on the other hand, the lack of market access facilitated agricultural extensification. In Bagëtia, it simply became too time and energy consuming to transport agricultural goods to and from the market. In Dardha, two factors were particularly important: first, the Macedonian market was inaccessible because Albanian farmers could not compete with the lower prices and better quality of Macedonian products; and second, the domestic market in Korça was inaccessible because of the long distance and the lack of adequate means of transportation. In both Bagëtia and Dardha, therefore, inadequate market access diminished land rents and pushed capital and labor out of agriculture.

Biophysical Conditions

Like market access, spatial variations in biophysical conditions (e.g., in soil fertility or precipitation) translate directly into the creation of land rent. David Ricardo has shown that if all other inputs such as labor and technology are kept equal, farmers with more fertile land capture more rent than those with less fertile land. Under the same circumstances, farmers who own the most fertile land get the largest share of rent, and those who own the least fertile land get none (1973 [1817]). Extending Ricardo's argument, farmers in villages with biophysical conditions that are more suitable to crop production capture larger shares of rent than farmers in villages where biophysical conditions are less favorable.

Differences in biophysical conditions among villages thus cause differences in rent creation. In each village, differences in biophysical conditions shape households' allocation of capital and labor between cultivation and livestock husbandry and between agriculture and off-farm activities in general.[10] In Kodra, Bagëtia and Dardha, these dynamics were clearly discernible. In Kodra, for example, biophysical conditions were suitable for intensive agriculture. The valley in which Kodra was located was fertile; the aspect of the slopes to the sun made them fit for vineyards; and a largely intact irrigation infrastructure provided the water necessary for intensive vegetable production. Although many households had invested capital and labor outside of agriculture, most had remained part-time farmers who combined subsistence production with small-scale, intensive commercial agriculture and off-farm activities.

In Bagëtia, on the other hand, biophysical conditions were much less favorable to intensive agricultural production. The cooperative had converted forests and pastures into arable land, which was largely unsuitable for cultivation. After the collapse of socialism, households began to shift capital and labor away from cultivation and toward livestock husbandry, and away from agriculture and toward emigration. Ultimately, one may regard the massive extensification of land use, which Bagëtia experienced in the postsocialist period, as a swing back to a more sustainable use of resources.

Just as in Bagëtia, biophysical conditions in Dardha were also unfavorable to intensive agriculture. Dardha's land was fertile, but the surrounding mountains were karstic and the soil did not hold water. The breakdown of the cooperative irrigation infrastructure facilitated the extensification of land use because it led households to shift capital and labor away from agriculture and toward seasonal migration and local, off-farm activities.

In sum, since the collapse of socialism, biophysical conditions, ethnicity and market access have determined the amount of rent available from land use and off-farm activities (in particular, migration). As a result, land users in Kodra, Bagëtia and Dardha reallocated their household capital and labor to those activities that potentially yielded the highest rent. The reallocation of capital and labor differed among villages depending on the particular configurations of ethnicity, market access and biophysical conditions. Land use changed in response and the result was intensification in Kodra and extensification in Bagëtia and Dardha.

Broader Socioeconomic Differentiation among Villages

The shifts in rent creation and distribution not only triggered processes of land use intensification and extensification. Together with the land use changes they produced, these shifts also led to a broader socioeconomic differentiation among the three study villages. I will now briefly examine three key indicators of this differentiation: income, productive assets and infrastructure, and political influence.

Income

Kodra, Bagëtia and Dardha had about the same average household income during socialism. The majority of adult villagers were members of the local cooperatives and received a relatively equal remuneration for their work. By contrast, in 2004, the villages had become markedly differentiated. Kodra was clearly leading in terms of average household income at 4,390 Euro per annum (p.a.). Kodra was followed by Dardha (3,480 Euro p.a.) and Bagëtia (2,775 Euro p.a.) (see Figure 5.1).

Not much of this income was generated in agriculture. In Kodra agriculture contributed only 17 percent to households' average annual income, compared

Figure 5.1. Average household income per village by source in 2004.

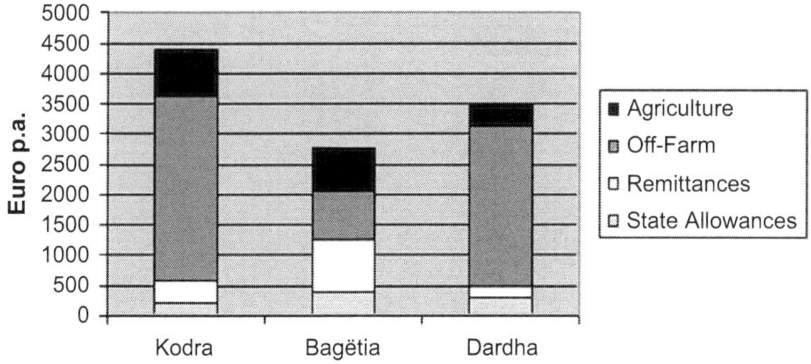

```
                                    ■ Agriculture
                                    ▨ Off-Farm
                                    □ Remittances
                                    □ State Allowances
         Kodra      Bagëtia     Dardha
```

Source: Household interviews.

to 24 percent in Bagëtia and 10 percent in Dardha. In Bagëtia agricultural income was thus relatively high, despite the extensification of land use that occurred when the villagers moved from cultivation to animal husbandry.

Yet, what explains the enormous differentiation of annual household income among the three villages is not income from agriculture, but rather income from off-farm sources.[11] In Kodra, off-farm sources contributed 69 percent to households' average annual income. In Dardha, they contributed 76 percent and in Bagëtia 28 percent. In Kodra, the largest part of this income was generated through employment in the construction and service sectors in and around Pogradec. In Bagëtia and Dardha, it was derived from seasonal labor migration to Greece and Macedonia.

Compared to the high level of income generated through off-farm sources, income from other sources, such as remittances and state allowances, amounted to a smaller fraction of the overall income. With a contribution of 32 percent to the average household income p.a., Bagëtia led the three villages in remittances – not surprising considering Bagëtia's high emigration rate. As the overall poorest village, Bagëtia also received most state allowances, while Kodra, the richest village, received the least.

Overall, the data on the amounts and sources of annual household income indicates a clear differentiation among the villages which did not exist under socialism.

Productive Assets and Infrastructure

A second indicator of the growing differentiation among Kodra, Bagëtia and Dardha is productive assets and general infrastructure. As described in Chapter 2, the villages' assets and infrastructure were similar during socialism. By 2004,

Table 5.3. Productive assets and general infrastructure per village in 2004.

	Kodra	Dardha	Bagëtia
Productive Assets			
Irrigation infrastructure	functional	dysfunctional	dysfunctional
Agricultural pharmacy	1	–	–
Tractors	1	–	–
Private Assets (% of households)*			
Washing machine	50%	100%	0%
Private cars	20%	20%	0%
Satellite dishes	1%	5%	30%
General Facilities			
Shops	4	2	2
Bars	4	2	–
Church/Mosque	2	–	1
Elementary school (8 years)	1	1	–
Car repair shop	1	–	–
Medical facility	1	–	–
Hotel	–	1	–
Gas station	–	2	–
Social Networks			
Farmer's Association	1	–	–
Credit Association	1	–	–
Rural Tourism Association	–	1	–
Forest User Association	–	1	–

Source: Direct observation, household interviews and (*) expert estimations.

they had become noticeably differentiated (see Table 5.3). Mirroring the distribution of income, Kodra was clearly leading the villages in amenities, followed closely by Dardha and then Bagëtia.

Political Influence

A third and final indicator of the growing socioeconomic differentiation among Kodra, Bagëtia and Dardha is political power. By 2004, the three villages had become noticeably differentiated in political importance. Dardha had lost its status as a regional political and intellectual center. After the collapse of socialism, many of the socialist elite who had taken up residency in Dardha (the former cooperative center) were forced to retire from their political positions. Kodra, by contrast, had been able to improve its political standing. In 2004, it was located in the same commune as Bagëtia, and it thoroughly dominated the commune council, which represented the commune's nine villages. The commune council consisted of thirteen representatives, five of which came from Kodra. Bagëtia and the seven other small villages each sent one representative to the council.

I use these three factors (villages' political influence, their average household income, and their productive assets and general infrastructure) to indicate the marked socioeconomic differentiation among them. This differentiation emerged after the collapse of socialism, under which all villages had shared relatively equal socioeconomic standards. The indicators reviewed above demonstrate that Kodra, the village with the best conditions for agricultural production, best off-farm employment opportunities, and most obstacles to migration, fared better in socioeconomic terms than Dardha and Bagëtia. Overall, the increasing socioeconomic differentiation among the three villages resulted from shifts in the creation and distribution of rent in conjunction with the changes in land use that those shifts produced.

This broader socioeconomic differentiation also mirrors the differentiation among Kodra, Bagëtia and Dardha in terms of land use. Land use became more intensive in Kodra and less intensive in Bagëtia and Dardha. Intensification and extensification were facilitated by three factors: ethnicity, market access and biophysical conditions. Since the collapse of socialism, the three factors have increased in importance in and beyond the study villages because they determined the rent available to land use, migration and off-farm employment. In reaction, (and in different ways in each village) land users shifted the allocation of capital and labor between agriculture and off-farm activities, causing land use to intensify in some and extensify in other villages. In the next chapter, I will examine the effects of changes in capital and labor allocation on spatial patterns of land use within villages.

Chapter 6

THE CRISIS OF CAPITAL AND LABOR: EFFECTS ON LAND USE WITHIN VILLAGES

The third pattern of land use change I examine is the intensification and extensification of land use within villages. As I have shown in Chapter 3, land use within villages had become more intensive in areas close to the village centers and less intensive towards the village fringes since socialist times. In this chapter, I argue that this pattern is the result of a widespread lack of access to capital and labor.

I begin the chapter by highlighting households' dependence on access to land, capital and labor in agricultural production systems in Kodra, Bagëtia and Dardha. I then examine how households gained access to the three production factors in 2004. I suggest that rental arrangements kept access to land flexible. However, access to capital and labor was scarce because, in agriculture, they were merely residuals from other, non-farm, economic activities such as employment in the local service sector or wage labor abroad. I argue that that since the collapse of socialism land users have concentrated capital and labor in areas generating the highest land rents. As a result, they began to cultivate areas near the village centers with more capital and labor intensive crops than under socialism. At the same time, they de-intensified production on their more distant plots.

The Dependence on Land, Capital and Labor in Agricultural Production

In 2004, agricultural production in Albanian villages was characterized by a mix of complementary and interrelated land use practices. Many farming households, for example, grew grapes and onions to generate cash income but produced other vegetables for subsistence consumption. Many cultivated wheat primarily to produce straw as winterfeed for their livestock. The degree of their engagement in one or another of these activities and the benefits they were able to derive from that engagement was primarily dependent on their access to land, capital and labor.

In Kodra, Bagëtia and Dardha, the villagers engaged in wide variety of agricultural practices. In 2004, the average household in the three villages used 0. 47 hectares of agricultural land. Of this, 0.27 hectares were cropland, 0.1 hectares vineyards, 600 square meters orchards and 400 square meters vegetable gardens. On average, each household owned one cow, seven sheep, two goats, half a pig and either one horse, mule or donkey. Access to land, capital and labor was crucial to households' agricultural production.

To produce grain, for example, households depended on access to land that was fertile and, preferably, irrigated. Capital was essential to buy seeds and pay for the cost of land preparation. In 2004, for example, hiring a tractor operator to plow, harrow and sow a field cost about 14 Euro per hectare. Hiring a combine harvester to later collect the harvest cost an additional 65 Euro per hectare. Compared with the profits available from grain production, these cost were considerable. Consequently, only 37 percent of grain producing households in Kodra, Bagëtia and Dardha hired the services of tractor operators to prepare their fields. Instead, the majority prepared their cropland in a much more labor intensive and less effective manner, using draft animals to pull plows and harrows (see Photo 1.1).

Like the production of grain, the production of grapes, vegetables and fruit trees required access to suitable land and a substantial input of capital and labor. Grape production, for example, called for sloped land and exposure to the sun. It also required about 20 labor days per 0.1 hectares for land preparation and grape harvest. Likewise, the production of vegetables was feasible only on irrigated land and was very labor intensive. For onions, for example, farmers calculated 60 labor days per 0.1 hectares for land preparation, planting and harvesting. Finally, the cultivation of fruit trees required high initial investments of capital. Rootstocks for apple and pear trees, for example, cost about 3 Euro in 2001, a substantial sum for farmers aspiring to grow an orchard.

Last but not least, livestock production required high investments of capital and labor. Compared to other land use practices, access to land was only a minor constraint because the villagers of Kodra, Bagëtia and Dardha had turned much of the cooperative cropland into common pasture and, thus, created abundant space for animal grazing. Access to capital and labor, however, was indispensable for engaging in livestock production beyond the subsistence level. For example, in 2003 Aleksander and Lindita Sherifi, a shepherd family from Kodra, bought purebred dairy goats for a price of 3,600 Euro by taking a credit from the Albanian National Savings Bank (brokered through an aid organization in Tirana). Like capital, labor inputs for livestock production were substantial. This was especially true when livestock production was combined with dairy production. In addition to shepherding, the Sherifis, for example, hand milked their goats twice a day. Substantial labor also went into the production of winterfeed.

This brief review of agricultural production in Kodra, Bagëtia and Dardha illustrates why the land use practices of households in rural Albania depended on access to land, capital and labor. I will now turn to an examination of the mechanisms by which the households gained, maintained and controlled access to the three production factors.

The Mechanisms of Access to Land, Capital and Labor

Land

Good quality land was scarce in Kodra, Bagëtia and Dardha. The average household in the three villages used 3.6 agricultural plots with an average size of merely 1,300 square meters. Despite the relatively egalitarian mode of land privatization in two of the three villages (Kodra and Dardha), households were nevertheless differentiated by their access to land. The household with the largest farm, for example, owned 1.4 hectares of agricultural land, while the household with the smallest farm only owned 0.1 hectares.

The solution for households that did not own sufficient land (or whose land was illegally occupied by pre-collectivization owners) was to rent land. Overall, 18 percent of households in the three villages were involved in informal land rentals, either by renting land in from others (13%) or renting land out to others (5%). The percentage was highest in Kodra, where almost one third of households were involved in land rentals. Land rentals usually occurred on cropping land and pastures (that were then used as hayfields), and to a lesser extent on vineyards.

Rental agreements were not usually documented in writing. Households often rented parcels from emigrated neighbors, paying in cash or production shares. The duration of rentals ranged from one season to several years. If the rental agreement exceeded more than one season, both the landowner and/or the renter could terminate the contract at the end of each harvesting season. For example, Bashkim Zela, my host in Kodra, rented 0.15 hectares of cropping land from Gjergji and Afërdita Proni, an elderly couple, who lived in the same village quarter (*lagja*) as the Zelas. The Pronis had four sons who were either living in Greece or suffering from poor health conditions that impeded their engagement in agricultural labor. When Bashkim asked the Pronis in 2001 if he could rent their plot (which then lay fallow), the two readily agreed. The parties settled on a rent payment of 56 Euro per year, leaving the crop choice to Bashkim.

As in this case, rent payments usually depended on the type of land that was rented out. In 2004, the rent for 0.1 hectares of cropping land, for example, was about 30 Euro per year. For the same amount of land in vineyards, the price exceeded 130 Euro, as in the case of Lefter and Vaçe Sherifi, winegrowers in Kodra, who rented in 0.3 hectares of vineyards from a household that had moved to the city of Vlora in the mid-1990s. As rent, Lefter and Vaçe paid one third of the annual production value of the plot (which was 1,200 Euro in 2003). Compared to the high rent payments for vineyards, the rent for pastureland was quite low. For 0.1 hectares, it varied between 16 Euro in Bagëtia and 20 Euro in Kodra. Aleksander Sherifi, the goat herder from Kodra, for instance, paid only 40 Euro per year for 0.2 hectares of pasture which he used to produce hay and corn for fodder. Aleksander rented the plot from a neighbor whose children were in Greece. The rental agreement had developed out of a minor conflict between Aleksander and the landowner. Aleksander occasionally had allowed his goats graze on the neighbor's land. The neighbor then told him to pay rent if he wanted to use it.

Overall, land rentals kept land tenure arrangements in Kodra, Bagëtia and Dardha flexible. Although a market to purchase and sell agricultural land did not exist in either of the villages, land rentals facilitated access for households in need of additional land.

Capital

As I have argued above, access to capital is a key factor shaping land users' production choices. Access to capital largely determines who can and who cannot benefit from land and other natural resources. Capital exists in many forms. It can exist as financial capital in the form of income, credit or savings, or technological capital in the form of agricultural implements.

In rural Albania, as elsewhere in the world, access to financial capital is especially valuable because it is versatile. Income, credit and savings can be converted into other access mechanisms (e.g., land, labor, etc.); they can be used for a direct fulfillment of basic livelihood needs (e.g., to buy food); and they can be transformed into socio-political influence (e.g., through providing credit). I will now explore the accessibility of income, credit and savings, and technology and information for households in the three study villages.

In Kodra, Bagëtia and Dardha, households gained access to financial capital primarily through off-farm sources. In 2004, the average household cash income was 3,550 Euro per year. The bulk of this was generated through local employment in the construction or service industries, or through seasonal labor migration (2,160 Euro). Agriculture was the second most important source of income (607 Euro), followed by remittances (480 Euro) and state allowances (300 Euro). The distribution of household income shows how large the disparity was between households. The richest 15 percent of households in 2004 earned more than 5,500 Euro per year (with a maximum of 20,000 Euro). At the same time, the poorest 15 percent of households earned less than 1,430 Euro per year (with a minimum of 620 Euro).

Compared to income, credit was a less important means for gaining access to capital. In 2004, credit was extremely scarce in rural Albania. Only 5.4 percent of households in Kodra, Bagëtia and Dardha had ever taken out a loan. Most of these loans were from Kodra's credit association. In addition, some had been taken from a Tirana-based micro-credit organization ("For the Future Foundation"). None of these loans, however, were ever from private banks, which were reluctant to deal with the small credit amounts that most Albanian farmers sought.[1]

Because credits were scarce, households had to rely on other mechanisms to accumulate capital. Interest-free loans from clan members were relatively common, but they rarely exceeded sums of 1,000 Euro. Many households, therefore, relied on stockpiling strategies to build up savings. The production of livestock was the most popular of these strategies. Another type of stockpiling strategy was investment into social relations to create mutual support networks. Marrying one's children into respectable and wealthy families was a particularly clear example for this strategy (cf. Gustafsson 2003).

In addition to income, credit and savings, access to technology and information were other forms of capital that were important to land users in Kodra, Bagëtia and Dardha. Like access to financial capital, access to these forms of capital was limited. Households' most common access mechanism to these forms of capital was membership in Kodra's farmers' association. The association had 150 member households who came from Kodra and six other villages including Bagëtia. As I have described in Chapter 4, the association cooperated with several aid organizations to improve livestock breeding and the marketing of grapes. In Kodra and Bagëtia, it distributed Holstein and Bruna Alpina cows, as well as several purebred races of sheep and goats. The association also trained villagers in animal care, agroecology, and the processing of dairy products. On the whole, however, access to agricultural equipment and expertise was severely restricted in households in all three study villages.

Overall, the capital that households in Kodra, Bagëtia and Dardha invested into agriculture was clearly a residual from investments in other fields. Mirroring a national trend, households invested primarily in housing or micro-enterprises, not agriculture (cf. Nicholson 2004). After years of experiencing material poverty under socialism, the households' first priority had been to improve their living conditions. To this end, one in every three households in Kodra, Bagëtia and Dardha had started building, or buying, new houses or apartments. In addition, one in every five households had significantly improved its old home. For another 28 percent of households, most investment occurred in the development of micro-enterprises outside of the agricultural sector. In other words, households invested outside of agriculture first. The residual income that they then invested in agriculture was either the money they gained from that investment or the remaining capital they had.

In short, households with access to capital invested primarily in housing or small businesses. The little that households invested in agriculture often barely covered the costs for seeds, fertilizer, land preparation or winterfeed.

Labor

Like access to land and capital, access to labor directly affected land use because it shaped farmers' freedom of production choices. In Kodra, Bagëtia and Dardha, as elsewhere in rural Albania, households' labor availability was severely constrained by the effects of migration.

In 2004, 60 percent of households in the three villages had at least one member permanently or seasonally working abroad. Seasonal migrants often spent up to nine months away from their homes. They stayed in their villages of origin only during the winter months, when agricultural production was at a standstill and demand for labor was lowest. Furthermore, the household members who migrated were typically young men and women between 18 and 35 years of age. As a result, many households lacked the labor power of the most productive age group for agricultural activities.

In addition to migration, labor was drawn out of agriculture through off-farm employment in the local service and construction sectors. Because of its low economic viability, agricultural labor had become increasingly unpopular with the younger generation, especially compared to emigration or seasonal migration. The following anecdote, told by a young migrant worker from Dardha, clearly makes the point:

> "After we harvested the wheat, my father went to pay the driver of the combine harvester for the work he had done. But [the driver] said: 'I should pay you because all you got is one sack of wheat.' So we spent about 200 Euro to plant the wheat and we only got 1,000 Lek [8 Euro, sic!] from it! Now, why should we plant wheat again?"

Finally, a substantial strain on labor availability in the three villages was related to households' educational strategies. In 2004, more than 33 percent of households had at least one member enrolled in either high school or university. Through their educational strategies, households were investing in capacities that they hoped would yield future income streams. Yet, a substantial amount of the households' capital and labor were absent because students who wanted to attend high school or university often left their villages of origin to reside in the cities and towns which had those facilities. High school students from both

Bagëtia and Dardha moved to the commune center or larger towns; for university, students from all three villages had to go to Korça, Tirana, or Skopje.

Overall, migration and educational strategies had led to the situation in 2004 in which the average household in Kodra, Bagëtia and Dardha had only three members between 14 and 75 years of age and, thus, able to contribute labor power to household production. To decrease labor shortages, households engaged in reciprocal labor exchange, especially in livestock herding. Hiring wage laborers, by contrast, was very uncommon. Households also relied heavily on the labor power of women and pensioners. With many men having sought work abroad or in the off-farm sector, the agricultural labor force in the three villages underwent a trend of feminization from 1990 to 2004.

To summarize, the analysis of access mechanisms demonstrates that households faced different constraints with regards to land, capital and labor. One the one hand, access to land was largely unconstrained, as households made extensive use of land rentals. Access to capital and access to labor, on the other hand, were key limitations to agricultural production. Mirroring a general trend in postsocialist Albania, households in Kodra, Bagëtia and Dardha experienced a massive outflow of capital and labor from agriculture into migration and off-farm activities (cf. King 2005).

Access to Capital and Labor and Land Use Outputs

The outflow of capital and labor from agriculture was directly linked to the kind and amount of produce farmers cultivated. Households with more capital and labor to spare invested more in agriculture and had higher land use outputs.

On average, households with higher incomes produced more grapes, planted more wheat and corn, and tended to keep more sheep and goats (see Table 6.1).[2] They also hired tractor operators to plow their land more often than households with lower incomes. Households that relied on tractors for land preparation used more than twice as much land as households that plowed with draft animals.

Like access to capital, households' access to labor was linked to their land use outputs. Households with higher labor capacities used more land, planted more wheat and corn, and harvested more grapes than households with smaller labor capacities (see Table 6.2).

Access to capital and labor were thus key factors influencing households' productive strategies and land use outputs. The better their access to capital and labor, the more land use outputs households generated. This clear correlation between access and land use outputs did not exist for other access mechanisms, such as access to authority, knowledge, or social networks.[3] In the following section, I will more closely examine the link between households' productive strategies and their access to capital and labor.

Table 6.1. Household income and land use in 2004.

Income p.a. (Euro)	Grape Yields (quintals)	Surface Wheat & Corn (ha)	Sheep & Goats (heads)
> 4.000	27.4	0.18	11.4
> 3.000	15.1	0.21	12.7
> 2.000	7.3	0.17	6.6
> 1.000	7.1	0.17	3.8
< 1.000	–	0.03	9.3

Source: Household interviews (n = 56).

Table 6.2. Household labor capacity and land use.

Members of Farming Households (Ages 14–75)	Grape Yields (quintals)	Surface Wheat & Corn (ha)	Land Area in Use (ha)
6 (n = 1)	27.00	0.80	1.10
5 (n = 2)	11.20	0.35	0.54
4 (n = 16)	15.69	0.14	0.48
3 (n = 13)	3.69	0.16	0.45
2 (n = 14)	4.82	0.09	0.37
1 (n = 4)	1.67	0.04	0.20

Source: Household interviews.

Access Differences among Households

In 2004, I could differentiate four categories of households in Kodra, Bagëtia and Dardha. The first group was households that had access to both capital and labor. The second group consisted of households that lacked capital but had access to labor. The third group were households that had access to capital but lacked access to labor. And finally, the fourth group consisted of households that lacked both capital and labor. Each of the four groups had its own, distinct production strategies.

The Sherifis – Access to Capital and Labor

When I became acquainted with the Sherifis – a full-time farming family from Kodra – in 2004, they operated a small winery and distillery (*mini-cantina*). Their household consisted of six people: Lefter and Vaçe Sherifi, an energetic couple in their 40s; their two sons, ages 8 and 14; and Lefter's parents, ages 70 and 65. Except for the small pension of Lefter's parents, the family made a living entirely on agriculture. Through their various farm activities they generated a yearly income of about 4,000 Euro. Thus, they belonged to the upper economic stratum of village society.

During socialism, Lefter had worked as a simple horse-cart driver for the cooperative. He liked his job and maintained an affinity for horses and other livestock. When the socialist system collapsed, the Sherifis began to specialize in raising sheep and cattle. Livestock, Lefter explained to me, had been in high demand after the time of the collapse. However, as the market for meat and dairy products consolidated and prices for fodder increased, animal husbandry became significantly less profitable. In 1996, the Sherifis sold their animals and Lefter went to pick peaches in Greece. When he returned after one season, the family invested their savings into the winery and distillery.

By 2004, the Sherifis owned 0.2 hectares of vineyards and rented an additional 0.3 hectares from a family who had left Kodra. On this land, they harvested some 70 quintals of grapes and they bought 15 quintals from their part-time farming neighbors. They sold their wine for 3.20 Euro per liter and raki for 4 Euro per liter. Selling wine and raki alone, the Sherifis earned an income of 3,600 Euro.

As a small addition to their income from wine and raki, the Sherifis produced vegetables for the agricultural market in Pogradec. In 2003, they harvested 60 quintals of onions on 0.15 hectares of fertile and irrigated land. On another 300 square meters, they grew a late variety of tomatoes. They sold the onions for 800 Euro and the tomatoes for 320 Euro.[4] In addition to growing grapes and vegetables as cash crops, they cultivated beans, cherries, apples, quinces, potatoes and corn for their own consumption. Each summer they bought a cow, which they fattened and slaughtered in December.

The Sherifis were one of the few full-time farming households in Kodra. Unlike most other households in the village, they planned to intensify their agricultural production in the future. Their largest, and most remote, plot of land was located on one of the steep hills at the village fringes. Because of its remote location and lack of irrigation, the Sherifis had never used it and let it turn into common pasture. By 2004, however, they were planning to bring it back into production and cultivate grapes. "Money [to buy rootstocks] is not the problem," Lefter told me. What had kept the family from investing into this plot had been tenure insecurity resulting from restitution claims by pre-collectivization owners. On the whole, the Sherifis represent households in Group 1, which have access to capital and labor. Access to these two essential productive resources allowed them to make intensive use of their land.

The Meksis – Lack of Capital and Access to Labor

The Meksis were a family in Bagëtia who lived on animal husbandry. Their household consisted of Vangjel Meksi (54 years old), his wife Lina (40 years old), and their two youngest sons, ages 18 and 16. Vangjel and Lina's two oldest sons had left the household in 1995 and 1996 to work as shepherds in Greece. They sent home whatever money their young families could spare at irregular intervals.

During socialism, Vangjel had been a cooperative guard and Lina had been a member of the agricultural brigade in Bagëtia. When the socialist regime collapsed, the young couple had to support their four small children and faced a difficult situation. Despite their hard efforts to raise livestock and grow wheat and corn, the family went through periods when there was not enough food to eat. Only as their children got older and the household's labor power increased, were they able to produce enough food to feed themselves and generate a small surplus.

With sufficient labor power, the Meksis were one of the few households in Bagëtia who used land relatively intensively. The family kept 30 sheep and goats, two cows, a pig, a mule, and about a dozen rabbits and chickens. On plots close to their home, they planted alfalfa, corn, sugar beets, beans, potatoes and other vegetables on 0.7 hectares. They left their fields at the village fringes (about 0.8 hectares) as common pasture, which they sometimes used to collect apples or wild plums from a few interspersed fruit trees.

Livestock and vegetable production provided the Meksis with a secure subsistence base and a modest source of income. For example, in 2004, the family slaughtered one calf and the majority of lambs and goat-kids for household consumption. They also kept all the wool and most of the dairy products for themselves. To generate cash income, they sold a bull for 640 Euro, a calf for 320 Euro, five lambs and goat-kids for 200 Euro, and about 50 kilograms of cheese for 120 Euro. Their income was supplemented by social assistance from the Albanian state which totaled 144 Euro for the entire year.

Overall, the Meksis exemplify a household in Group 2, with access to labor but a lack of capital. Compared to households in Group 1, these households used land less intensively but were still engaged in agriculture as a livelihood strategy.

The Geris – Access to Capital and Lack of Labor

Like the Meksis, the Geris were from Bagëtia. They were a family of six: Andis and Monda Geri, a couple in their late 20s; their three children, ages six, five and three; and Andis' 61-year old mother, Valbona. By Bagëtia's standards, the Geris were well off. For about three months each year, Andis picked lemons, oranges and olives in Greece. There, he earned 30 Euro for an eight-hour day, plus 15 Euro for two hours overtime. He stayed with his emigrant brother and, therefore, had low expenses for room and board. Every season Andis was able to save up to 3,000 Euro.

Because Andis was absent from Bagëtia for much of the agricultural season, the Geris lacked labor power. When Andis was not there, Monda and

Valbona took care of the children and a flock of 80 sheep. The two women generally took turns shepherding in a collective arrangement with another household from their village quarter (*lagje*). At the end of each summer, when Andis returned from Greece, he harvested hay on two hectares of land, cut oak shrub, and bought barley in the lowlands as winterfeed for the sheep. The household did not cultivate any crops.

In 2004, the Geris sold 60 lambs. Through this, they generated a household income of about 2,500 Euro. Like most households in Bagëtia, they invested their capital outside of the village. In 1998, they had bought an apartment in Pogradec for 22,500 Euro which they rented out to tenants. By 2004, they began weighing the option of moving permanently to Pogradec. According to Andis, the decision depended on how their children would do in school. Until then the children had only spoken Vlach, and if they did not learn adequate Albanian in Bagëtia's elementary school, the family would have little choice but to leave the village. In this case, Andis foresaw, they would have to abandon livestock production and he would have to spend more time working in Greece.

Overall, the Geris represent households in Group 3, which have access to capital but lack labor power. In comparison to households in Groups 1 and 2, households such as the Geris do not use land very intensively. For them, agriculture often generated only supplementary income, or was used to produce goods for subsistence consumption only.

The Shumkas – Lack of Capital and Labor

In Dardha, the Shumka household consisted of 45-year-old Drita Shumka and her thirteen-year-old son. Drita's 52-year-old husband Sterjo and their three daughters lived in Monastir, Macedonia, where Sterjo worked either as a bricklayer or hired laborer in agriculture and their daughters went to high school and university. Each school month the Shumkas spent more than 500 Euro – all their income – on the education of the children.

Although the girls had moved permanently to Monastir, Sterjo came home to Dardha for the winter months. Except for during these months and other rare stints when Sterjo was able to come home for two or three days, Drita took care of all farm activities. The Shumkas owned one hectare of agricultural land in Dardha, plus one cow, thirteen sheep, two goats and a donkey. Relying only on Drita's labor power, they used their land at a very low level of capital and labor input. They left 0.15 hectares of their land as common pasture and used another 0.2 hectares to harvest hay. During the cooperative times, these plots had been irrigated and cultivated intensively with wheat, corn, beans and tobacco.

Except for a grape plot and a small vegetable garden, Drita cultivated only one plot of land. With 0.35 hectares, that was the household's largest plot. It was planted with wheat, corn and beans in rotation. Like all cropland in Dardha, the plot was not irrigated and was low in productivity (4 quintals of wheat in 2004), but it did yield straw and corn as feed for the Shumka's livestock. As additional fodder, Drita harvested hay and bought three quintals of bran per year. She usually sold one calf per year, but kept all wool, dairy products and meat for their own consumption. Drita herded livestock in the typical collective arrangement in which neighbors take turns shepherding.

The Shumkas' most economically viable plot was their vineyard of 0.2 hectares. In 2003, Drita and Sterjo had harvested 20 quintals of grapes on this plot, which they used to make wine and raki. They sold the raki to a bar owner in a neighboring village. They needed the income generated to survive the winter months when Sterjo could not find work. When I lived in Dardha in 2004, the village's grape production was close to zero because the grapes had been infested with mildew (*vrug*). Drita told me that with this important source of income missing, making ends meet and paying for their children's schooling was to become even more difficult.

The Shumkas exemplify households in Group 4, that lack access to both capital and labor. Compared to households in all other groups, these use land least intensively.

In sum, the portraits of the Sherifi, Meksi, Geri and Shumka families suggest that access to capital and labor had a profound influence on households' production strategies. Aggregate data from 53 household interviews in Kodra, Bagëtia and Dardha corroborates this observation (see Table 6.3).[5]

Table 6.3 shows that households with access to both capital and labor (Group 1) harvested more grapes, planted more wheat and corn, and used more land than all other households. Households that lacked the two factors (Group 4) harvested the least amount of grapes, had the least amount of small ruminants, and used the least amount of land. In between the two extremes, households that lacked either of the two factors engaged in diverse agricultural production that included both capital and labor intensive and capital and labor extensive strategies. For example, households lacking access to capital (Group 2),

Table 6.3. Production strategies according to household group in 2004.

Household Group	Grape Yields (Quintals)	Surface Area Wheat & Corn (ha)	Sheep & Goats (Heads)	Land Area in Use (ha)
1 (n = 19)	13.39	0.21	9.79	0.86
2 (n = 16)	5.56	0.21	4.44	0.53
3 (n = 9)	4.89	0.06	16.78	0.38
4 (n = 9)	3.33	0.12	3.44	0.33

Source: Household interviews.

compensated by engaging in the labor intensive production of grapes, wheat, corn, or vegetables. Households lacking access to labor (Group 3) compensated by engaging in land use activities that required relatively little labor input, such as animal husbandry (for meat, rather than dairy production).

Spatial Patterns of Land Use within Villages

I will now examine the spatial patterns of land use resulting from households' diverse production strategies. Following Johann Heinrich von Thünen's argument that land rent decreases with distance from a farmstead (1966 [1826]), one would expect a spatial pattern of land use that resembles concentric rings around each village. As land rent decreases with distance from the village center, von Thünen predicts land use will become increasingly less intensive as distance from the village increases.

The spatial pattern of postsocialist land use in Kodra, Bagëtia and Dardha was largely congruent with von Thünen's prediction. In all three villages, land use in 2004 was most intensive at the village center and decreased in intensity towards the village fringes (see, for example, Photo 6.1).

Photo 6.1. Land use of Stiljan and Plaguna Tane from Dardha.

Sources: IKONOS-Image 09-21-2003 and interview with Stiljan Tane 10-21-2004.

Generalizing land use, agricultural production at the village centers of Kodra, Bagëtia and Dardha was devoted to vegetable and milk production (from cows kept in sheds). Away from the village centers, less intensive agricultural crops like corn and wheat were planted, followed by hayfields and animal husbandry on pasture and in coppice. The outermost ring of land use was occupied by forest, which the villagers used for timber and firewood extraction.

This pattern of concentric rings around the villages emerged as the result of the flexible land tenure arrangements and household production strategies described above. Households, such as that of Lefter and Vaçe Sherifi, in which both capital and labor were accessible, tended to use all their land as intensively as possible. The households invested their capital and labor into commercial vegetable production and vineyards. They also had incentives to continue to use their plots at the village fringes as orchards or hayfields.

The second type of household, such as that of Vangjel and Lina Meksi, lacked capital but had sufficient labor power available to work the land. Households in this category engaged in diverse production, including both intensive and extensive agricultural strategies. They used their central plots intensively, cultivating vegetables, grapes and grain either for subsistence production or for the market. They used their more remote plots at the village fringes either for fodder production or as grazing land for their livestock.

The third type of household, such as that of Andis and Monda Geri, had access to capital but lacked labor power. Households in this category used all their land at a very low level of intensity. The households often abandoned their plots the village fringes or used them as pastureland for their livestock. On plots closer to home, they cultivated vegetables, fruits, or grapes for subsistence production. At times, they rented out plots to households of full-time farmers.

Finally, the fourth type of household, such as that of Drita and Sterjo Shumka, lacked both capital and labor power. Compared to the three other types of households, the agricultural production of households in this category was the least intensive. These households de-intensified land use on their plots at the village fringes and kept only a few plots close to their homes under cultivation. Women and pensioners did most of the agricultural production in these households. Unused plots were sometimes rented out to households that had the capital and labor power to pay for and work them.

Taken together, households' production strategies shaped the pattern of intra-village intensification and extensification. The spatial layout of land use in Kodra, Bagëtia and Dardha was structured in concentric rings around the village centers. The rings decreased in land use intensity the further they moved to the village fringes. This distinct layout of land use emerged despite differences between land users' access to key productive resources. Households with higher capital and labor capacities were able to use land more intensively than households who lacked the two resources. However, the differences among households were mitigated by widespread informal land rentals which kept land tenure arrangements flexible. Thus, even if a household could not use one of its plots in a certain circle of land use intensity for lack of capital and/or labor, other households with access to these resources could fill the gap by renting the plot. Since the early 1990s, land users in all categories had de-intensified production on plots at the village fringes because of the general constraints on capital and labor availability in rural Albania. These plots were not only further away from their homes, but also often less fertile or located on steep terrain.

One exception existed to the general pattern of land use intensity decreasing towards the village fringes: the cultivation of grapes. Unlike the production of other capital or labor intensive crops, grape cultivation did not occur at the village centers. Instead, vineyards were located either completely at the village fringes or at a medium distance between the village center and the village fringes. This exception may be explained by the fact that grape production, more than the production of any other kind of crop in rural Albania, depends on biophysical conditions such as slope, terraces and exposure to the sun, conditions found more readily at the villages fringes than at the village centers.

In sum, within villages access to land, capital and labor set the parameters for households' decision-making about land use. Although households were clearly differentiated in their access to these productive resources, all strove to concentrate capital and labor in areas close to the village centers which generated the highest land rents. The spatial outcome of their endeavor has been the pattern of concentric rings of land use intensity described in Chapter 3.

.

Chapter 7

THE FATE OF THE POSTSOCIALIST FOREST

In late August 2004, Klodian and I accompanied our friend Gjergji Hoxha to cut fir stanchions in the Guri Nikes and Qafë Panje forest sector. On Gjergji's mules, we crossed the thick coppice and underbrush surrounding Bagëtia to the north until we reached the vast stretch of deciduous forest that extends from Qafë Panje to far beyond the Shkumbin River. By the time we made it through the coppice, we were all soaking wet from the waist down because the branches had brushed the morning dew into our clothes. We rode like this for several hours through the late summer woods.

Gjergji, who was leading the excursion, made sure to stay on barely visible paths and never left the cover of the forest. Klodian and I had become acquainted with him around a campfire one evening at the ruins of Bagëtia's cultural center. Gjergji was twenty-one, muscle-packed, and, except for his older brother, the only man of his age still living in Bagëtia. He worked in Greece for a few months as a teenager, but his Muslim family name kept him from obtaining the legal status his Vlach neighbors enjoyed. Fed up with making a haphazard living abroad, Gjergji decided to return to his family and try his luck in the illegal timber and firewood trade emerging in the Gorë and Mokra mountains. He quickly learned the rules of the game and became an expert logger. Unlike most woodcutters I knew in Guri Nikes and Qafë Panje, he did not cut trees for firewood but specialized in cutting high value timber from old growth oaks and fir trees. Overall, this was physically less demanding, but it required covering large areas of forest in pursuit of suitable trees.

After about three hours on the mules, the three of us arrived at the place that Gjergji had in mind. On the way, we had run into groups of unlicensed woodcutters twice and heard chainsaws at a short distance with greater frequency. Until then the ride had felt like a Sunday excursion, but now Gjergji was determined to get some work done quickly. As Klodian and I hobbled the mules, he got the chainsaw ready and felled an impressive mountain fir about twelve meters tall. He removed the branches and cut three two-meter pieces from the log. Finally, he halved them into six stanchions, each about 20 to 30

Photo 7.1. Gjergji Hoxha loading fir stanchions onto his mule.

Photo: Stahl.

centimeters thick. The entire chainsaw operation did not take more than 20 minutes. Afterwards, the heavy stanchions had to be loaded onto the mules. Klodian and I offered to help, but we moved so clumsily that Gjergji preferred to do it alone. He had his own clever technique for doing so. Bringing a stanchion up vertically behind the mule, he would slowly lower it onto a V-shaped rope, tied at its ends to the saddle and held open horizontally by a strong, crutched stick (see Photo 7.1). When the stanchion was cradled on the V, he could securely tie it to the saddle. For balance, he loaded each mule with two stanchions.

When the mules were ready, we headed back for Bagëtia. Several times on the five hour trek back home, the animals threatened to collapse under their heavy loads. Gjergji explained that they would need at least one day of rest after today's exhaustion. Economically, our trip had paid off for him. The following week he sold the stanchions, along with others he and his brother had cut in the weeks before, for 8 Euro each to a firewood and timber trader from the lowlands. It is likely that the stanchions ended up as door or window frames or as stanchions on construction sites.

Gjergji's story is not unique in Albania today. Like he, hundreds of small-scale, unlicensed woodcutters roam the Qafë Panje and Guri Nikes forest sector. Thousands more cut firewood and timber in forests elsewhere. The rushing of people to exploit forests started immediately after the collapse of socialism. Since then, the rush has moved from the easily accessible forests of the lowlands to the more difficult to reach woods of the highlands. In its wake, it has left severe forest degradation.

In this chapter I examine the rush on forests through case studies in Kodra, Dardha and Bagëtia. I argue that with the collapse of socialism the state's grip on forest resources loosened dramatically. The power vacuum has created rent-seeking opportunities for a broad set of social actors. Unlicensed woodcutters like Gjergji, timber and firewood merchants, large-scale logging companies and corrupt Forest Service officials all compete over rents from forest resources. They all fear losing out if others happen to harvest an area first.

Albanian Forests after Socialism

Forests are arguably Albania's most valuable natural resource. Overall, they occupy more than 1 million hectares – more than one third of the country's land surface. The growing stock is estimated at 89 million cubic meters, of which almost 50,000 cubic meters per year are extracted as high value timber and industrial roundwood.[1] Rural people also depend heavily upon forests to secure their livelihoods.

The vast majority of Albanian rural dwellers are dependent on firewood as their primary source of energy for cooking and heating. According to the official data from the Directorate General of Forests and Pastures, Albania's yearly demand for firewood is 452,724 stacked cubic meters (INSTAT 2005). In reality, however, the number is likely to be much higher. Experts from the District Forestry Service estimate that the annual amount of firewood used in the district of Pogradec alone exceeds 100,000 cubic meters – and Pogradec is just one of 36 Albanian districts! Estimating that 70 percent of Albania's population of 3 million is dependent on firewood consumption and approximately use between 1–2 cubic meters per capita per year, the annual firewood extraction at the national level most likely exceeds 2 million cubic meters, corresponding to 2–3 percent of the standing volume in Albania.

The importance of forests to rural livelihoods, however, goes beyond the use of firewood. Most households generate additional benefits from forest resources through forest grazing and the collection of non-timber forest products such as medicinal herbs and pine resin. In many rural areas, woodcutting is the only opportunity for local employment and one of the main factors reducing poverty and emigration.

Ironically, the distribution of forest ownership does not reflect the importance of forest access to rural dwellers. After the collapse of socialism, the new democratic government legislated that forests be restituted to historical owners. However, at the time of collectivization in 1944, only 6.4 percent of forest was privately owned (while 92 percent was state-owned and 1.6 percent officially communally-owned). As a result, little forest has been subject to restitution. To further concentrate control over the forest in the hands of the state, the postsocialist government's commitment to restitute property rights to forest proved to be weak. Consequently, by the late 1990s, virtually all of Albania's forest continued to be in state ownership.[2]

At the same time that it did not restitute ownership rights to forests, the Albanian state tried to strengthen its control over forests. In 1992, Parliament passed the Law "Concerning Forests and the Forest Service Police" (Forest Law), which regulates the administration, development and treatment of the forest stock, its exploitation and protection, the organization of the Forest Service, and enforcement provisions.[3] The government passed the Forest Law against the objections of external forestry experts who believed that keeping the forest in state ownership would lead to large-scale abuse by the Forest Service. The Forest Law was also contested by local authorities who proposed a stronger recognition of customary use rights instead of state ownership (de Waal 2004). The Forest Law remains contested to this day. There is a staggering discrepancy between its stipulations and actual forest practices. For example, to prevent forest exploitation, the Forest Law grants licenses to interested individuals

(Article 25) and requires a special permit for the transportation of forest products confirming that the extraction occurred legally (Article 31). Yet in practice, licensed woodcutters and transporters account for a small fraction of the actual extraction. In some districts, such as Mirdita, forestry experts estimate that up to 95 percent of the wood cut annually is felled illegally.[4]

In sum, the Albanian state has attempted to establish control over access to forest by prolonging restitution and instituting strict forest legislation. Arguably, it has done so to create and appropriate rents from forest resources. However, its attempts have failed as the discrepancy between the de jure and the de facto situation in Albania's forests indicates. I will now examine the local dynamics leading to this failure.

Peasant Resistance and Custom in Kodra's Chestnut Forests

The rush on resource rents characterizing postsocialist Albanian forest relations started immediately after the socialist regime collapsed. Kodra's valuable chestnut forests were among the first forests loggers targeted. There, rent-seeking was joined by another motive for forest clearing: peasant resistance.

The Destruction of "Communist Trees"

The orgiastic wave of vandalism that shook the Albanian countryside at the end of the socialist regime may be explained by the negative meaning that most rural dwellers associated with the cooperatives. In Kodra, loathing for the political and economic system was no different than elsewhere in rural Albania. In the final days of the regime, villagers from Kodra went on a rampage to unmake the cooperative by destroying its major assets. Alone and in small groups, villagers sneaked out at night to loot and destroy the cooperative's infrastructure. The cooperative's irrigation system, for example, was thoroughly dismantled; the concrete plates covering the irrigation channels were stolen and later found in homegardens and on the terraces of farmhouses. (The system was rebuilt in the 1990s with funds from USAID). Likewise, the villagers looted the cooperative's five large animal shelters and carried off their bricks for private construction purposes. Most of the cooperative's fruit trees were cut down, and the valuable timber was sold through middlemen to entrepreneurs in Greece.

The initial destruction of cooperative's assets soon gave way to the destruction of anything associated with the socialist regime. In the wake of this massive destruction, significant portions of Kodra's chestnut forests were cut down. Ironically, these forests had not been part of the cooperative but were held in state ownership and previously managed by the District Forest Service (i.e. the regional branch of the Directorate General of Forest and Pastures, a state agency under the Ministry of Agriculture). Like looting the cooperative's buildings and irrigation infrastructure, cutting the "communist trees" was not merely the villagers' expression of their frustration with socialism. Nor was it simply a way for rural dwellers to profit economically. It was, above all, an act of political resistance with the goal of eliminating any possibility that the socialist regime could recover and assert control over production again.

Yet, within this general turmoil in Kodra, there was also another type of reaction. In fact, many villagers opposed what they regarded as the senseless destruction of common property. Cutting the chestnuts evoked especially strong feelings among those who had owned chestnut plots prior to collectivization. In reaction, some of them began guarding their ancestral patches, patrolling the land or camping out at night to keep loggers away.

Customary Forest Management

In 1992, the villagers who had previously tried to protect their ancestral forest plots, decided to officially claim control over these plots on the basis of historical ownership. They felt encouraged to do so by appeals by the local government to villagers to protect "their" chestnut forests against wanton destruction.

The villagers took the local government's appeal as encouragement to restitute the chestnut forests to their pre-collectivization owners. The village elders still remembered the old borders, and it was easy for those entitled by customary ownership to claim property rights to their ancestors' chestnut parcels. After more than thirty years of collectivization, many original families who claimed rights to chestnut parcels had grown into extended families (*fis*), but this was not problematic because the families divided the parcels among all member households in an egalitarian manner. As a result, households received 0.3 hectares on average, the largest parcel measuring one hectare. About 40 percent of households did not receive any chestnut trees in the process, as they could not claim historical rights. This inequality did not diminish the general acceptance of the restitution, however, as virtually all villagers recognized the legitimacy of historical claims – even those who did not receive any forest.[5]

Despite the villagers' efforts to protect their patches of chestnut forest, the trees did not fare well between 1990 and 2004. This was due not only to the chestnut forest's partial destruction in 1991, but also to the chestnuts' more recent affliction with *endothia parasitica*, a decease locally referred to as "chestnut cancer." As a result, Kodra's chestnuts – once a prized, regional specialty famous throughout Albania – have lost much of their economic value.

The inability to benefit from the tree crops has motivated many villagers to cut down their chestnut trees for firewood or timber. Mustafa and Paulina Drini are one of the families who cut down their chestnuts trees. The couple is in their early 40s, and they are full-time farmers who can barely make ends meet. The family owns one of the oldest houses in Kodra with a well that is said to be over 250 years old. When I met the two in 2004, Mustafa told me that he was originally from Korça and had moved to Kodra 21 years ago after marrying Paulina. The household's claim to a chestnut plot of about one hectare stems from Paulina's side of the family. This was a clear exception to the patri-linearly biased Albanian inheritance practices. It was possible because Paulina's father was living with the couple until his death in 2003. From 1993 to 2002 Mustafa and Paulina harvested 2–3 quintals of chestnuts each year and sold them for about 0.64 Euro/kg (in 2002). In 2003 Mustafa cut the old trees, which had become cancerous, and harvested seven cubic meters of timber of which he sold three for a total of 220 Euro. At the time of our interview, he was looking for a buyer for the rest of the timber. The young trees growing on the plot were not yet productive. To speed up the growth, Mustafa and Paulina regularly cleaned up the plot by cutting blackberries and removing the brush and undergrowth. Their story underscores the relative value of chestnut wood, especially for poor households, yet also shows that the absolute benefits that villagers are able to derive from chestnut forests are quite modest. For Mustafa and Paulina, who hold one of the largest plots in the village, the benefits amounted to less than 200 Euro per year over the last decade and a half (including timber sales).[6]

In sum, the restitution of Kodra's chestnut forests and their customary management offer more general insights into the relations governing forests in postsocialist Albania that may help explain the pattern of forest degradation. The story of Kodra's chestnut forests demonstrates the general absence of the rule of law in Albanian forests in the early 1990s. For local actors, the restitution of the de jure state-owned chestnut forests was possible for two central reasons: First, the restitution of the chestnut patches was widely perceived as legitimate within Kodra; the residents perceived the distribution of benefits from chestnuts as relatively egalitarian. Second, there was little interest in the village's chestnut forests outside of Kodra. The absence of interest from outsiders, including the Forest Service, can largely be explained by the low rents arising from control over these largely depleted forests.

Anarchy and Communal Management of Forest in Dardha

The Destruction of Forest in the Anarchy of 1997

As in Kodra, much of the cooperative infrastructure in Dardha was destroyed in the upheavals of the system change in 1991. The most damage to Dardha's forest, however, occurred during the months of anarchy in 1997. That year, Dardha – like most other settlements in rural Albania – was drawn swiftly into the national turmoil. In the years after the system change, the road passing through Dardha developed as one of the main routes for running contraband between Albania and Macedonia. In the anarchy of 1997, the smuggling, crime and violence in the area (which was hardly kept below the surface in the years before) came out into the open. 1997 was both an extremely dangerous time in Dardha and also one that provided great opportunities. Some villagers profited indirectly from the contraband trade. A few others were actively engaged in it.

I spoke with two active smugglers, Dragan and Darko Shumka, brothers who ran fruits between Macedonia and the Albanian city of Elbasan. When I talked to them in 2004, they still dreamed about the 250 Euro profit they made on an average trip. However, they still had nightmares about how their business ended in 1997. Bandits had tried to stop their truck at gunpoint in an attempt to take their goods. When the two refused to stop, the bandits started firing Kalashnikovs. A bullet hit Dragan in the right calf, and Darko was hit in the shoulder. A third passenger, and friend of the two, was hit in the spine and died in the hospital in Korça a week later. The driver's cabin of the truck still stands in Dardha, full of some sixty bullet holes.

Macedonia reacted to the violence and crime spreading from Albania into its territory by closing its Albanian border. During much of 1997, therefore, it was impossible to run contraband. Smugglers and truck owners had to find alternative occupations. With all state control vanished, many soon started to cut trees along the border road. The wood was transported to the lowlands of Korça and sold as firewood. Within a few weeks, the cutting took on the dimensions of a gold rush.

Agron Andoni, a bar owner from Dardha, referred to the period from March 1997 (when logging started) to early 1998 (when it ended) as golden times. Each day, he hosted 30 – 40 truck crews at his small bar. Each time a crew went out to the forest, the men would first stop at his place and buy a case of beer. When they came back, they would stop by again to eat. At the time, Agron sold 30 kg of fish a day and still could not meet the demand. Some logging crews, he recalled, even went out to cut even twice a day. Cutting occurred during the day and night until at least 2 a.m. While some of the truck crews cut the firewood themselves, others bought it pre-cut by others. Crews used vehicles ranging from trucks, minivans, trailers, to horse carts for transportation.

Buying up wood from individual loggers was a lucrative business. Before they were wounded in the hold-up, Dragan and Darko also worked in this trade. The two brothers transported firewood for 5–6 months. They bought the wood from individual loggers for 6 Euro per cubic meter and sold it in Korça for twice as much. Their IFA truck held 11–12 cubic meters, thus resulting in a profit of about 65 Euro per trip.

Nevertheless, Dragan and Darko and bar owners like Agron were the exception; the rents available from logging did not accrue to villagers from

Dardha. Less than half a dozen villagers participated in the cutting of wood. Their number fell even further after masked men assaulted one of the villagers and stole his chainsaw. After this episode, all inhabitants of Dardha stayed close to the village even to herd livestock. The logging frenzy ended in early 1998 when civil order was restored in Albania. By that time, 262 hectares of Dardha's valuable old-growth forest had been reduced to shrub and coppice. The logging occurred primarily along the road from Korça to the Macedonian border where forest access was easiest and land rents were the highest.

Communal Forest Management

Since 1998 all commercial logging activities in Dardha have ceased. In 1996, Albania's Ministry of Agriculture and Food passed Regulation No. 308, transferring usufruct and managerial rights to forest and pastures to participating communes.[7] To facilitate the transfer process, the Ministry established the Communal Forest and Pasture Management (CFPM) project. The project, supported by the World Bank and USAID, aimed to improve the management of Albania's forests by increasing the interest and participation of local communities and administrations. Its long-term goal was to transfer rights to 40 percent of Albania's forests to communes. It also provided funds for rehabilitating forest areas close to villages in order to meet the firewood and fodder requirements of the local population (DGFP et al. 2002).

The commune in which Dardha is located began participating in the CFPM project in 2001. Stimulated by examples from other communes, it made a request to the Directorate General of Forest and Pastures to participate in the devolution program. In reaction, the parties negotiated a contract that transfers use and managerial rights to the commune of Dardha for 10 years. The contract grants local users the right to use forest pasture and cut firewood and fodder. It expects the local administration to set aside forest land for protection and rehabilitation. It specifies the transfer of rights to 3,742 of the 13,000 hectares of forest land located within the commune boundaries. Ironically, most of this area consists of low value coppice. In Dardha, it is made up exclusively of the 262 hectares of forest degraded in 1997.

Before the transfer contract was signed, the village councils decided how to use and manage the devolved forest. In Dardha, as in the other villages of the commune, the council opted for communal management rather than individual, family-based arrangements, in part, because villagers recalled the quarrels about the privatization of agricultural land and were afraid of conflicts resulting from boundary transgressions on individualized forest plots. Many also feared the responsibility and the investments necessary in an individual arrangement.[8]

The council's decision in favor of communal management again illustrates that the devolved forest was generally considered to be of little value. Most villagers from Dardha already had stable livelihood strategies based on seasonal labor migration and subsistence agriculture. The necessary labor to exploit the devolved forest on an individual basis was thus tied in other, more profitable, livelihood strategies.

Rent-Seeking in Dardha's Coppice

In a final step before the transfer of use and management rights, the village council had to approve a management plan. The council hired a private forest consultancy to draft it for a total of 13,600 Euro. The commune's newly founded forest and pasture user association (*shoqatë e përdorimit të pyjeve dhe kullotave*) assisted the consultancy. The management plan divided the communal forest into six management units that correlated with the territories of the six villages located within the commune. The plan also specified the state of the forest in 2001 and laid down the rehabilitation goals until 2011. After it was approved, the forest user association assumed management of the communal forest.

The association consisted of eleven board members elected in a meeting with the commune council and the chairpersons of the commissions the association established in each village.[9] The association was financed, in part, through fees that the commune charged villagers for the right to use the communal forest. These fees were generally low. The right to cut the yearly supply of firewood for one household, for example, could be obtained for 4 Euro (Photo 7.2). The annual fee to cut oak twigs (used for winterfeed) was 1.60 Euro. Using forest as pasture cost 4.80 Euro per head of cattle or 0.80 Euro per head of sheep or goat. The low fees not only reflected the association's non-profit orientation, they also reiterated the low economic value of the remaining forest resources in Dardha.

Yet, if village elites and powerful actors in the commune anticipated high political rents in return for communal control over the devolved forest, they were not proven wrong. For example, Rako Dautovski, who became the chairman of the communal forest user association, has been able to capture significant power from his position. A former cooperative agronomist, Rako was originally from a village next to Dardha. He was able to gain support in all villages of the commune by building up a clientele among the villagers. To build up his following, he used the financial and political resources available to him through his position as chairman.

In October 2004, for example, Rako organized an information seminar and invited several people from Dardha. The seminar, "Regulations Regarding Communal Forests and the Participation of the Population Therein", was funded and co-organized by a non-governmental organization specializing in the development of mountain zones. The seminar, which I attended, was scheduled to start at 9:00 a.m. and end at 5:30 p.m. In fact, it started at 9:30 a.m. and ended

Photo 7.2. An old man from Dardha hauling firewood and fodder from the communal forest.

Photo: Stahl.

at 10:36 a.m. Instead of the scheduled eight and a half hours, it lasted only one hour and six minutes. Rako hand-selected the twenty villagers who were present at the event. One of them was the cleaning lady at the elementary school where the seminar took place; the others were pensioners from Dardha. After 68 minutes, each of them received 8 Euro, the equivalent of the salary for a day's work as an unskilled laborer in construction.

As a local patron, Rako had a strong influence over the association's employment decisions, specifically at the managerial level.[10] In 2004, the association employed about half a dozen forest technicians and several forest guards. The technicians identified the areas open for firewood and fodder extraction and carried out forest rehabilitation tasks. They started reforestation on seven hectares and thinning and pruning on 25 hectares of Dardha's forest (see Photo 7.3). At Rako's recommendation, two elderly ladies were hired as forest guards in Dardha. The two usually sat at the main path leading into the forest and rarely caught villagers who cut firewood or oak twigs without having paid the obligatory fees. Because the communal forest is too depleted to be attractive for commercial loggers and the remaining parts of the original old-growth forest high up in the *Mali i Thatë* Mountains are inaccessible, all large-scale illegal logging activities in Dardha have ceased. Therefore, rent

Photo 7.3. Protected afforestation area in communal forest near Dardha.

Photo: Stahl.

extraction through unlicensed logging has come to a complete halt. Yet, as the case of Rako Dautovski illustrates, even a degraded forest still offers opportunities for political and economic rent-seeking.

In sum, the rampant logging in 1997 and the subsequent process of forest devolution offer valuable insights into postsocialist forest relations that may help explain the pattern of forest degradation in Albania. As in Kodra, the logging in Dardha started at a time when state control had vanished. The loss of control facilitated the appropriation of rents by illegal loggers and other actors who profited from the rush on forests. When state control was restored in 1998, the logging frenzy ended. However, at that time it had already reduced the value of the forest resources to such a degree that the rents available to the state had become insignificant. For the state, the transfer of use and managerial rights to the commune a few years later was therefore little more than a way of feigning compliance with the wishes of the country's international donors. Nevertheless, the devolution of rights did make some rents available to local actors. On the one hand, rents arising from control over communal forests became available to powerful actors in the forest user associations and at the communes. More generally, rents became available to all members of the forest user associations, albeit mostly in the form of the symbolic value arising from having input in the management of local resources.

Massive Logging and State Corruption in Forests Around Bagëtia

Let us now return to the vast forests around Bagëtia, known as the Qafë Panje and Guri Nikes forest sector, where we accompanied Gjergji Hoxha to cut fir stanchions. The villagers of Bagëtia, like their peers in Kodra, claimed property rights to the forests surrounding their village when the state's power eroded in the early 1990s. Although they had never enjoyed statutory ownership rights to the forest prior to collectivization, they now asserted claims based on historical use that they should be the only ones entitled to use the forest. Their claims did not meet much opposition in the initial years. During the turmoil of 1991, for example, Bagëtia did not experience external pressure by extra-legal loggers, largely because of its remote location. Yet, their claims also went by unheard by the Directorate General of Forests and Pastures, which retained Qafë Panje and Guri Nikes under formal state control.

Like Dardha, Bagëtia was drawn into the nationwide anarchy of 1997. That year, massive logging began in the forests above the village when loggers from the neighboring village of Kumbull cut trees in a portion of the forest claimed by Bagëtia. Because they far outnumbered the people of Bagëtia, there was little that the residents of Bagëtia could do to stop them.

In the years following 1997, the logging expanded to other areas, involving an ever-growing number of people from villages in the entire region. Since then, every summer when the dirt roads have dried and become passable for large four-wheel drive trucks, hundreds of loggers come up the mountains to cut firewood and timber. According to the former director of the District Forest Service in Pogradec, the volume of wood extracted increased from 35,000 cubic meters in 1990 to 55,000 cubic meters in 2004. As a result of this massive increase in wood extraction, the forests above Bagëtia degraded dramatically between 1990 and 2004 (see Chapter 3).

Antecedents: A Tradition of Timber Poaching

On a much smaller scale, timber poaching has occurred long before 1997. Even during socialism, state control over the forest resources at Qafë Panje and Guri Nikes was not absolute.

For over twenty years, Maks Dulellari, for example, added to his meager salary by poaching fir stanchions (*kollonat*). In moonless nights Maks, who worked as a simple woodcutter for a state enterprise in Qafë Panje, cut the stanchions and transported them along hidden paths with his mule to his customers in the lowlands. These trips were extremely dangerous and often took him all night. If Maks had been caught, he would have disappeared in a forced labor camp for many years. Although he never told anyone about his business, the activity could not be kept secret in a small village like Bagëtia. Maks, therefore, always traveled at a fast pace, making sure he never used the same road twice.

Despite its danger, poaching *kollonat* had been a profitable business. The price of the stanchions depended on their thickness, which usually ranged between 20 to 30 centimeters. Buyers had paid about 5 Lek for each centimeter of girth. Thus, by making three to four trips each summer month, Maks Dulellari had earned up to 1,000 Lek a month – three times the salary of a regular cooperative worker.

Actors, Conceptions and Practices in Logging

Timber poaching during socialism took place on a very small scale, but unlicensed timber and firewood extraction from 1997 onward exhibited as in Dardha the characteristics of a gold rush. When I was living in Bagëtia in 2004, the rush was still in full swing. The atmosphere was loaded with conflict, as several kinds of actors collided in their quest for forest rents. In their collision, rivaling conceptions of property rights to the forest resources at Qafë Panje and Guri Nikes came to the fore. These conceptions shaped the forest use practices villagers, forest authorities, logging companies and unlicensed loggers.

First, villagers from Bagëtia regarded the vast areas of forest as the village's common property. They justified their claims by pointing to customary rights based on historical ownership. They argued that during the 18th century Bagëtia had played an important role as a settlement along the *Via Egnatia* and that the village had historically owned land far beyond its present location. To mark their claims, the villagers sprayed warnings on trees and rocks all over the forest territory: "Property of Bagëtia" (*Prona e Bagëties!*) or "Don't touch Bagëtia's forest!" (*Mos prek pyllin e Bagëties!*).

Forest authorities, on the other hand, perceived the forest sector of Qafë Panje and Guri Nikes as state property. The Directorate General of Forests and Pastures had issued legal concessions to six companies for logging in the area and considered all other ongoing logging activities as illegal. To enforce its claim, the Directorate General ordered forest guards from the District Forest Service in Pogradec to patrol the sector. Yet, as elsewhere in Albania, the chronically under-financed district officials lacked the capacity to enforce that control. In total, therefore, only nine forest guards were patrolling the entire Qafë Panje and Guri Nikes area. For a monthly salary of 100 Euro, each was supposed to control between 2,500 to 3,000 hectares. Although most had been working for the Forestry Service since socialist times, many possessed strong allegiances to the rest of rural society and, as a result, often felt the tug of local loyalties. For example, because the entire District Forest Service in Pogradec commanded only two off-road cars (of which one was permanently used by the director), forest guards had to hitch rides with legal, or more likely *illegal*, firewood traders to travel to Qafë Panje. Under these conditions, it was not surprising that most forest guards showed considerable leeway in deciding when to enforce or *not* enforce forest regulations.

The six logging companies that had obtained concessions from the Directorate General of Forests and Pastures based their claims to forest resources on the fact that they had followed the legal stipulations for forest exploitation. In order to be eligible for a concession, the company owners had to prove that they did not have criminal offences on their record. They had also won a tendering process that granted them concessions for 6-month periods. In theory, the companies had to follow strict regulations stipulating where to cut and how much volume to extract. In practice, however, the regulations were handled very loosely. According to the regulations, for example, the Forest Service had to mark the trees the concessionaires were allowed to cut. Yet, despite this rule, the concessionaires often took unmarked trees and got away with it by bribing Forest Service officials.

The concessionaires strongly resented the presence of loggers without a concession. As the loggers did not pay for a license, they were able to sell firewood and timber at a lower price. The concessionaires considered this unfair competition and used it to justify why they habitually extracted larger volumes than permitted by the Service.

Unlicensed loggers saw the timber and firewood of Qafë Panje and Guri Nikes as open-access resources. They negated the claims of Bagëtia, the Forest Service, and the concessionaires by pointing to their natural right to subsistence. Everyone, they reasoned, should have the right to ensure a secure livelihood. As one elderly man, who was caught cutting trees for firewood, yelled at a forest guard:

"Okay, fine me if you want! I have five children who cut trees; fine them too, if you want to! Start the prosecution! We will all go to jail and the state will have to feed us. Do you think we came here for fun? We came here because we have to eat!"

The subsistence argument, indeed, carried some weight with forest officials. When I interviewed the director of the District Forest Service in Pogradec, he frankly admitted: "In the past the Directorate has been a bit lax with loggers around Bagëtia because we knew that they are poor and need the forest as a source of livelihood." The argument also was convenient for him because it provided an acceptable explanation of why the Service failed to enforce the law.

Photo 7.4. IFA-truck loaded with poached firewood from Qafë Panje.

Photo: Stahl.

Like Gjergji Hoxha, most unlicensed loggers in Qafë Panje and Guri Nikes operated on a small-scale basis. They cut trees with chainsaws and transported the logs with horses or mules to places along the forest roads where the wood was chopped and picked up by firewood traders with IFA trucks (see Photo 7.4). The traders were usually small-scale entrepreneurs from the lowlands who often brought their own crews. In terms of the volume of extracted wood, the crews by far did the most damage to the forest in Qafë Panje and Guri Nikes. The crews usually consisted of four to six young men who were unable to find other work in their villages of origin. Each of them usually sold the wood he cut to the truck owner for the same price that the truck owner would pay to small-scale, individual loggers. By carrying a crew, however, the truck owner was not dependent on the fickle supply of wood from individual woodcutters.

Conflicts Among Forest Users

The different claims to the forest and the practices associated with each claim led to serious conflicts among forest users. One fault line ran between unlicensed loggers and the Forest Service. While the Forest Service usually left small-scale woodcutters alone, traders and logging crews, or "organized contraband" (in the jargon of the officers), were its preferred targets. In cooperation with the police (*policia rrugore*) the Service had obtained a list of truck owners in the district (including their names, residences, and license plate numbers). About 100 individuals, mostly from the lowland villages around Pogradec, were listed.

I therefore estimate that several hundred small-scale individual woodcutters, traders and logging crews were active in Qafë Panje and Guri Nikes. Finding it impossible to prosecute so many "poachers" at once, the Forest Service decided on a deterrence strategy. For example, on one day in August 2004, it initiated a concerted action involving all nine forest guards and the director, and fined unlicensed loggers in Qafë Panje, confiscating their timber and firewood. The volume of confiscated wood was so large that military support was needed to transport it to Pogradec. This action was part of a broader campaign to deter the unlicensed wood trade. Acknowledging that the lack of staff and vehicles limited the means available to the Service, it sought to at least heighten the perceived risk of detection. As the director of the District Service explained to me, "fear guards the graveyard."

As this story illustrates, keeping out unlicensed traders and logging crews was not easy for Forest Service officials. Sometimes it was even dangerous. In early 2004, for example, a violent scuffle ensued when a forest guard attempted to fine an truck driver near Qafë Panje. The driver believed the guard wanted to hitch a ride to the lowlands and had opened the door only to see the guard filling out the slip for the fine. The furious driver started yelling profanities, jumped out of the truck, beat the guard, and left him in a ditch next to the road.

Violent conflicts like this also occurred between loggers and the villagers of Bagëtia. In August 2004, a 20-year old shepherd had to be transported to the military hospital in Tirana after being beaten by a logging crew. He lay at the brink of death for several days. The conflict originated because the IFA truck carrying the crew had been trespassing on the shepherd's pasture. To protect the pasture and to teach the loggers a lesson, the shepherd and his father had placed a camouflaged nail board across the IFA's path and waited in a blind until the truck drove across the board. When the diver and his crew got out of the cabin and saw two flat tires, they started cursing and shouting insults that provoked the young man to leave his hiding spot. The heavy argument that ensued then turned into violence.

Fortunately, violence was not always a consequence of forest conflicts. Often a compromise could be reached between actors by either paying a bribe or involving customary authorities as mediators. Gjergji Hoxha provided one account of conflict resolution by bribery. About a year before we met, Gjergji had been making stanchions when he was caught red-handed by a forest guard known to both of us. The noise of the chainsaw had given him away, and he could neither run nor talk himself out of the trouble. Gjergji cautiously offered a bribe. "Come on," he said to the forest guard, "let's find a common language!" When the guard initially displayed some reluctance to accept the bribe, Gjergji insisted: "Come on, you are not a Serb, you are an Albanian. It *must* be possible to find a common language!" And, indeed, they found it. Instead of a fine of several hundred Euro, the two settled on a bribe of 8 Euro.[11] When Gjergji raised doubts about whether the guard would honor their agreement, the guard reassured him: "Are we men [of honor], or what are we?" (*Jemi burra o ç'farë jemi?*).

Resolution through mediation is another option for solving forest disputes nonviolently. In April 2004, when I was living in Kodra, a conflict between the Forest Service and an unlicensed trader was peacefully resolved through the mediation of an influential elder. In this case, a high-ranking Forest Service officer caught Dani Sherifi, a young firewood trader transporting a truck full of poached wood to the lowlands. The officer began to chase the truck with his off-road car. The wild chase ended in Kodra, Dani's home. There, the young man stopped the truck and ran off on foot. While fleeing, he saw a group of elders sitting in a bar. One of them was my host, Bashkim Zela. Dani approached Bashkim and asked for his help. Bashkim knew the officer from high school, and he promised to intervene on Dani's behalf. When the officer arrived with several forest guards, Bashkim tried to convince them to let Dani go. After a long discussion and a lot of *raki*, the Service officials finally agreed and gave the offender until midnight to sell the firewood. Otherwise, they threatened, he would be fined 4,000 Euro (approximately the value of the truck and its load).

The Distribution of Benefits from Unlicensed Logging

The stories of bribing Forest Service officials expose a general lack of accountability within the Albanian public administration (Saltmarshe 2001). Rent-seeking by way of controlling access to forest resources is common among officials at all levels of the Albanian Forest Service (cf. de Waal 2004). Unlicensed traders who are experienced in the business often have accumulated both the capital to bribe and good enough connections to be protected by officials high up in the Service hierarchy.

The villagers of Bagëtia, on the other hand, reap only a small share of the overall benefits from unlicensed logging. In 2004, just one household in the village – that of Gjergji's parents, Agim and Shegë Hoxha – derived substantial income from logging. The Hoxhas were the only Muslims in Bagëtia. Unlike their Vlach neighbors, they were easily recognized as such by their last name and, thus, could not obtain the usual 3-year visas for Greece. Like Gjergji, his brother had tried short stints at labor migration but always returned from Greece after just a couple months. Without household members working abroad, the Hoxhas had the most labor power available in Bagëtia. With a yearly income of over 13,000 Euro, they were also by far the wealthiest in the village. As the director of the elementary school in Kumbull, Agim Hoxha was one of the few villagers in Bagëtia who held an off-farm job. However, the logging activities of the two sons provided the family's main source of income. In 2004, they contributed some 6,000 Euro to the household's earnings.

Unlike the Hoxhas, the vast majority of other households in Bagëtia did not engage in commercial logging, nor did they benefit from the rush on forests in any other way. On the contrary, most of the benefits available from logging accrued to logging companies and unlicensed traders and crews from the lowlands, outsiders to the community.

The logging company of Fatos and Tomorr Shkurtaj, for example, had been in business since 1993. In 2003 and 2004, the two brothers held a concession to 15 hectares of forest in Qafë Panje and Guri Nikes. They owned three IFAs and a Mercedes truck, which they used to haul and deliver firewood. (Fatos liked to say that he had bought the Mercedes in Germany personally.) The Shkurtajs sold about 3,500 cubic meters of wood per year to private households, small merchants, and public offices. The selling price per cubic meter was 16 Euro. Production costs, they explained, amounted to 11.20 Euro per cubic meter, including cutting (5.60 Euro), transport (2.40 Euro), and taxes and fees (3.20 Euro). The logging company thus gained 4.80 Euro per cubic meter, amounting to an annual profit of about 17,000 Euro.

Compared to licensed logging companies, unlicensed traders and their crews operated on a much smaller scale. The number of unlicensed companies, however, exceeded that of licensed logging companies by factor 15 to 20. Dani Sherifi from Kodra, for example, had been in the business since 2003, when he bought a truck with the money his father had saved up for ten years as a taxi driver (3,200 Euro). Dani usually took three or four teenagers up to Qafë Panje where they cut firewood all day and returned at night. Occasionally, he also bought firewood from small-scale woodcutters who had permanent camps up in the mountains. The prices Dani paid his crew were the same traders paid throughout Qafë Panje. A crew member or independent woodcutter received 8 Euro per cubic meter. The price Dani obtained for selling the wood varied depending on the final destination. Villages closer to the forest paid less than those further away. Prices were especially high in villages located along the national road where the traders ran high risks of being caught. In Kodra, for instance, Dani sold the cubic meter of firewood for about 16 Euro. His IFA carried a maximum 13 cubic meters. On each trip during the season (May to October), therefore, he made a profit of about 70 Euro (40 Euro per roundtrip for gasoline already subtracted). In slightly more than half a season in 2003, Dani had sold 200 cubic meters, amounting to a total profit of 1,100 Euro.

Taken together, the actions of the actors in forest exploitation have caused the degeneration of forest resources on a massive scale. In fact, the data I presented here indicates that the loss of forest was even larger than the national forest cover data (discussed in Chapter 3) suggests. While the forest cover data reflects only the permanent removal of forest cover (i.e. deforestation), the real issue at hand is forest degradation (i.e. the permanent reduction in quality and quantity of forest growth).

Struggles Over Rent

In sum, the contestations about control over forest resources in Qafë Panje and Guri Nikes provide important insights into the political economy governing forests in postsocialist Albania. The disputes clearly demonstrated the state's inability to establish sufficient authority over the forest resources in question. In fact, the state appeared to be one of many actors making property claims to forest. These actors grounded their claims in either state law (Forest Service and concessionaires), customary regulations (villagers), or moral entitlements (unlicensed loggers and traders).

Furthermore, unlike in Kodra or Dardha, the forests around Bagëtia had high economic value and, therefore, made substantial rents available for capture. The attempt of the Forest Service to establish control over forest access and keep unlicensed woodcutters at bay, for example, must be understood as rent-seeking on the side of the Albanian state. At the same time, local Forest Service officials also engaged in rent-seeking efforts. Due to their (partial) control over access to forest, they were able extract rents in the form of bribes from concessionaires and unlicensed loggers and traders. Finally, unlicensed loggers and traders were able to appropriate shares of the value created in the forests of Qafë Panje and Guri Nikes. Relying on extra-legal access mechanisms, they obtained rents amounting to the sum licensed logging companies paid to obtain concessions.

In essence, the contestations over property rights in forests around Bagëtia were disputes over the distribution of value. Because of the high rents at stake, none of the local actors had yet managed to institutionalize their property rights claims. The lack of recognition of either of the claims resulted in anarchic property relations reminiscent of those in Kodra in 1991 and Dardha in 1997.

Chapter 8

RENT FROM THE LAND

In this book, I used rent as an analytical lens to examine patterns and causes of land use change in southeastern Albania. I have argued that the fundamental political and economic changes that occurred in Albania since the collapse of socialism profoundly affected the mechanisms through which rent from land and other productive resources was created and distributed among differently positioned social actors. The shifts in rent creation and distribution changed rural people's incentives and decisions about land use and caused land use change. Thus, I demonstrated both that rent is an aggregate force shaping society and environment, and that using rent as a lens to examine environmental change is a powerful analytical strategy for understanding human-nature interaction in postsocialist countries such as Albania and beyond.

Shifting Rent Dynamics and Land Use Change

Throughout this book I used rent dynamics to explain how broader political and economic processes affected social and environmental change in Albania. I identified four distinct patterns of land use change in Albania. The patterns must be understood as reflections of the country's broader political and economic transformation. The first pattern, the fragmentation of land use, is characterized by the dissolution of large physical structures – terraces, irrigation and drainage systems, the collective plot structure, etc. – which had been in place under socialism. The dissolution of these structures resulted from shifts in the creation and distribution of rent available to collective action. Economic liberalization and the transformation of the Albanian state from an authoritarian power to one in permanent political crisis shifted incentives for collective action away from the production and toward the marketing sphere. The associated shifts in rent creation and distribution motivated land users to alter the collective land use practices which had created and maintained these large physical structures under socialism.

The second pattern, intensification and extensification of land use *among* villages, was shaped by differences in ethnicity, market access and biophysical conditions. After the collapse of socialism, the three factors determined the rent available to land use vis-à-vis other economic activities, especially migration. At the village level, the three factors shaped land users' production strategies and, depending on their particular constellation in a given village, facilitated land use intensification in some villages and land use extensification in others.

The third pattern of land use change, intensification and extensification *within* villages, resulted from shifts in the supply of capital and labor available to land use. After the collapse of socialism, land users concentrated capital and labor in areas generating the highest land rent. They began to cultivate areas near the village centers with more capital and labor intensive crops. Concurrently, they de-intensified production on their more distant plots. The spatial pattern resulting from these dynamics is characterized by concentric circles of land use intensity within villages – intensity declines the further land use moves towards the village fringes.

Finally, the fourth pattern, forest degradation, resulted from shifts in control over access to forest resources. As the grip of the postsocialist state on forests loosened, a wide range of actors filled the resulting power vacuum. Typically through extra-legal practices, these actors managed to capture large shares of the rent that had formerly accrued to the socialist state. The rush on forest resources in postsocialism resulted in a massive degradation of Albania's forest resources.

Taken together, the four patterns of land use change can be explained by changes in rent creation and distribution which resulted from Albania's broader political and economic transformation. Since the collapse of socialism, decollectivization and the opening of Albania to movements of goods, capital, and people profoundly changed the mechanisms through with actors gain, maintain and control access to land and other productive resources. The changes in access mechanisms, along with changes in rural land and resource values, facilitated the shifts in rent creation and distribution, which, in turn, changed land users' incentives, land use decisions and practices.

The dramatic changes in land use I described demonstrate the power of rent as an aggregate force shaping society and environment. I have argued and shown that using rent as an analytical lens provides a powerful tool for understanding human-nature interaction in many resource fields. In the Albanian case analyzed here, using rent as an analytical lens yielded new insights and results. In particular, the focus on rent brought to light surprisingly different dynamics in agriculture and forestry. In agriculture, rents have decreased, motivating the majority of land users to withdraw from commercial production and instead practice low input subsistence farming. In forestry, on the other hand, large shares of rent suddenly became available to actors who were previously excluded from forest exploitation. Unlike in agriculture, from which capital and labor were withdrawn, the rents provided by forests proved so attractive that forest exploitation even pulled in capital and labor from outside of forestry. This book explored the social and environmental consequences of these differential dynamics in-depth. Through my analysis, I have shown that using rent as a lens to examine social and environmental change works equally well in different resource fields. In fact, one may argue that directing attention to agricultural dynamics alone (as most studies of postsocialist rural transformation do) generates, at best, a partial understanding of how the broader political and economic changes of postsocialism have affected rural society and environment.

In sum, the evidence I presented suggests that refocusing political ecology analyses on rent dynamics is a powerful strategy for furthering our understanding of how broader political and economic processes affect social and environmental change. Because postsocialist political economies have undergone profound transformations and the associated shifts in rent creation and distribution have been very pronounced, they may be especially suited for analyses of this kind. However, using rent as an analytical lens to examine social and environmental change can also provide valuable insights in postcolonial or post-authoritarian settings, contexts more frequently studied by political ecologists.

Rural Transformation and Albania's Accession to the European Union

On 12 June 2006, just 15 years after the collapse of socialism, Albania signed a Stability and Association Agreement with the European Union. On 3 April 2008, it was officially invited to join the North Atlantic Treaty Organization (NATO). Both steps must be regarded as milestones in Albania's journey towards EU integration. Although its speed of entry into the Union will depend on its performance, it is likely that Albania will achieve full integration within the next 15 to 20 years. A key question will then be how EU integration affects the land use patterns and practices I examined in this book. Drawing on the findings about the patterns of land use change, I am tempted to speculate about the changes that will occur:

Without doubt the process of EU integration will profoundly affect the political and economic dynamics shaping land use in Albania today. Already, the Stability and Association Agreement commits the country to intensify political and economic reforms to meet the EU's conditions. The reforms will strongly influence the creation and distribution of resource rents. For example, in return for pursuing the reforms, the EU has committed to integrate Albania into the European market. With respect to agriculture and forestry, this will create rents, for example in the form of EU subsidies, to be captured by land users and other actors. In this way, successful EU integration may bring about a more equal footing for Albanian farmers vis-à-vis their European competitors. It may even result in the return migration of many Albanians who, over the past 15 years, left the rural parts of the country to escape from poverty, desolate infrastructure, and lack of employment opportunities. Already, many migrants have invested their earnings in their villages of origin with the intention of returning in the future (Nicholson 2004). For return migration to occur, however, the non-agrarian sector will have to provide many more employment opportunities than it does at present. Yet, if this enormous obstacle can be overcome, the implications for rural land use would be dramatic.

Although not all return migrants are likely to be active in agriculture and forestry, their investments – together with EU-financed infrastructure – will greatly alter the face of the landscape. Within villages, growing urbanization will dramatically raise land rents at the village centers, likely pushing agricultural production out to the outer edges of the villages, and causing a re-intensification of land use at the village fringes. At the regional level, the current division between villages with intensive land use and villages with extensive land use is likely to harden. People and capital will not spread equally over rural areas. Instead, they will be concentrated in certain places where biophysical conditions and access to productive resources generate the highest rent. Land use extensification is, therefore, likely to continue in the more remote villages until the complete abandonment of cultivation is reached. Finally, regarding forests, degradation is likely to continue in the immediate future. In the face of the high rents and with powerful interests at stake, it seems likely that by the time EU integration will be achieved, much of Albania's remaining old-growth forest will have disappeared.

As this admittedly speculative scenario illustrates, to see how Albania's rural landscape continues to evolve and change in the process of EU integration will be a prodigious field for further research. As an analytical concept, rent has provided a powerful lens for understanding Albania's postsocialist rural transformation in the past and present – it will also be a useful tool for future research.

NOTES

Chapter 1. Introduction

1 To protect identities, "Kodra," "Bagëtia" and "Dardha," the names of all surrounding villages, and the names of all villagers are pseudonyms.
2 By land use change, I mean the physical change of land cover by human action on the surface of land.
3 Scholars in the Ricardian and Marxian tradition agree on this point but see Tribe (1977), Fine (1979, 264) and Harvey (1982, 353ff) for Marx's modifications of the Ricardian rent concept.
4 Examples of rent-seeking by those who control access to land and other productive resources abound. In Peru, for example, absentee landowners extract rents from smallholders through leasing and sharecropping arrangements or unpaid labor services (Deere and de Janvry 1979). In sub-Saharan Africa, social networks controlling access to scarce productive resources extract rents from farmers in form of the financial obligations that come along with network membership (Berry 1993). In Bulgaria, "sharks" controlling agricultural markets levy rents from smallholders by forcing them to sell their crops below a fair price (Giordano and Kostova 2002). Finally, in Albania, politicians controlling access to public property capture rents in the form of votes from squatters on state farmland outside of Tirana (Voell 2003, de Waal 2004).
5 The distinction between rights-based and structural and relational access mechanisms is a reaction to the privileged analytic center that legalistic notions of property rights have gained in many environmental studies (e. g., Hardin 1968, Ostrom 1990, Bromley 1991). In contrast to the latter, Ribot and Peluso make the case that property rights may not be sufficient to guarantee that rights holders will benefit from the resources to which they are legally entitled. From their point of view, property rights are just one among many mechanisms by which actors gain control over resources. Rather than being solely about 'rights' to resources, access is about actors' "ability" to derive benefits from them. For a similar argument, see Leach, Mearns and Scoones (1999).
6 For other illustrative examples of rent-seeking along a commodity chain, see Ribot (1998) on charcoal in Senegal, and To and Sikor (2009) on timber in Vietnam.
7 For example, one of the strongest proponents of individual ownership rights, The World Bank, argues that: "Clearly defining land rights during land reforms is key to improving the lives of poor people – farmers and nonfarmers alike (2001, cited in Sturgeon and Sikor 2004)."
8 Similar monopolistic market structures are described by Zbierski-Salameh (1999, 198–202) for Poland. She shows how socialist procurement centers, the largest buyers of agricultural products in the country, kept their monopolistic market control even

after they had been privatized. As their competitors were kept weak through tax disincentives and high risks involved in the specialization on retail, procurement centers alone were able to dictate the purchasing price of agricultural products.
9 For another example on how the setting of the baseline date for restitution excluded ethnic minorities from landownership, see Verdery (2003).
10 Thomas Sikor (2006) argues that the risks and obligations connected to ownership may turn assets into liabilities and reduce people's ability to derive benefits from land and resources to which they have legal titles. Examining how farmers in Poland and the Czech Republic have reacted to the obligations tied to landownership originating from legislation for environmental protection, Sikor finds that landowners in both countries see environmental obligations as threats to their ability to benefit from their land rights. In response, farmers seek to dissociate the rights of ownership from its obligations. Intending to increase the former and reduce the latter, they resist environmental legislation through open protest and hidden forms of non-compliance. From a rent perspective, they attempt to withstand the extraction of rent (in the form of environmental taxes or services) by states that control access to production opportunities.

Chapter 2. Albanian Socialism

1 The figure for the bunkers, exaggerated in most accounts, is from Hashi and Xhillari (1999).
2 Sjöberg (1991, 85) offers different figures. He speaks of 170,000 hectares distributed to 70,000 poor or landless families. Sjöberg's description of the Agrarian Reform also differs slightly from Mathijs'.
3 "1946" according to Sjöberg (1991, 106).
4 As a consequence of the pro-natalist policy, land per capita had actually dropped by 10 percent by the 1980s – despite the extension of arable land. In 1989 only 0.2 hectares per head of the population were available for cultivation (Sjöberg 1989, 8, cited in de Waal 2004, 20).
5 Rather than turning their livestock over to the cooperative, however, many peasant families chose to slaughter their animals instead (de Waal 1995).
6 On the concept of everyday resistance, see Scott (1985) and Peluso (1992). According to Scott, in the constant struggle between the peasantry and those classes that seek to extract rents from them, peasants have developed an repertoire of "weapons" which require little or no planning or coordination, which are often borne out of individual self-help, and which typically avoid direct confrontation with authorities. This repertoire is embedded within specific historical and environmental circumstances (Peluso 1992), and is based on notions of morality, rights, criminality and subversion specific to the peasantry (Scott 1976). The repertoire of resistance contains many different forms such as malicious gossip, character assassination, slander, foot dragging, false compliance, feigned ignorance, pilfering, and, at a later stage, desertion, dissimulation and sabotage. According to Scott, it is mainly through these forms of everyday resistance that the peasantry has defended its interests against both conservative and progressive elites. Seen over the long run, and compared to the brief and heroic, yet foredoomed instances of revolt, this constant, grinding everyday struggle has been more significant and more effective. It is largely in this way that subordinate classes make themselves noticed at the macro-political level.

NOTES 123

7   Despite the widespread dissatisfaction among the rural population, the elections of March 1991 were won by the Socialists. Ironically, it was the rural dwellers that secured their victory. The rural constituency voted predominantly for the Party of Labor while the oppositional Democratic Party won in almost all urban districts. The opposition explained its defeat in rural areas through a lack of media representation and psychological pressure on rural people to vote socialist. Probably the most crucial factor, however, was the widespread belief that the Democratic Party would privatize and restitute the collectivized land to the pre-war landowning class (Vickers and Pettifer 1997, 58). The Socialist government, however, did not last for very long. Ongoing strikes, demonstrations and vandalism forced it to resign after only two months in power. In June 1991, an interim coalition was formed in which Socialists, Democrats, and three smaller parties were represented. The interim coalition government ended in March 1992 and the following elections were won by the Democratic Party.
8   The Vlachs are known under many names including Aromanians, Aromani, Cincari, and Macedo-Romanians. Some scholars find different definitions for these names and the people they intend to represent, while others use them interchangeably. Among the Vlachs themselves, there is a variety of currents. The Aromanian Association "Union für aromunische Sprache und Kultur" in Freiburg, Germany, promotes the use of the ethnonym "Armîn" to stress the Vlachs' separate identity from the Romanians. In Albania, many Vlachs call themselves *Vlleh* or *Çobenj* (Shepherds). Today the Vlachs number about 200,000 people in all Albania (Schwandner-Sievers 1999).
9   Together, these villages today count some 4,500 people whose origin in the region dates back to the medieval Bulgarian and Serbian empires (Apostoli 2002). Their language is a Macedonian dialect closely related to Bulgarian. After cutting ties to former Yugoslavia, the villages are now successfully re-establishing socio-economic relations with the Former Yugoslav Republic of Macedonia (FYROM), which seceded from Yugoslavia in 1991.
10 For examples, see Humphrey 1983, Thelen 2003, Verdery 2004.
11 The term "shortage economy" was coined by Kornai (1980).

Chapter 3. Patterns of Land Use Change

1   I conducted participatory mapping to get village-level spatial representations of land use change. Mapping took one day in each village. It involved groups of six to ten villagers who were particularly knowledgeable about land use in 1990 (the year before the collapse of socialism) and/or 2004 (the year I conducted fieldwork) (e.g., farmers, shepherds, woodcutters, agronomists, former cooperative brigadiers, etc.). On large printouts of QuickBird™ and IKONOS™ satellite images, I asked the representatives to name localities, identify the boundaries of communal land use areas and individual plots, and classify land use into suitable categories. After common agreement was reached among the participants, we fixed names, boundaries and categories on transparencies laid over the printouts. Next, the participants identified the changes in land use since 1990, which then again were fixed on the transparencies. After the meeting with villagers, Daniel Müller, a GIS expert at Humboldt University Berlin, and I manually transferred the results into a Geographic Information System (GIS) through on-screen digitizing. We used this to develop full-blown land use maps. In addition to the spatial data obtained through the mapping, the discussions among the participants conveyed valuable information on local rules of land use, land reform implementation,

and property relations. For a very useful manual on participatory mapping, see Müller and Wode (2003).
2 Kodderitzsch (1999, 23) speaks of an even more drastic plunge to merely 80,000 hectares in 1993.
3 The production figures presented in this section are from key-informant interviews with former agricultural brigadiers in Kodra, Bagëtia and Dardha (for 1990) and production statistics obtained from the agricultural offices at the communes (for 2004).
4 Contemporary hybrid corn seeds were more productive than the seed used by the cooperative. However, they were also more expensive and difficult to find. Farmers, therefore, tended to select their new seed from the corn production of previous years. Contemporary hybrids, however, dramatically lose their productivity after about three years.
5 Agrotec's Albanian National Forest Inventory (ANFI) is based on the visual interpretation of Landsat TM and ETM mosaics from 1991 and 2001. Results from a village survey from four districts conducted in 2004 by the Junior Research Group on Postsocialist Land Relations from Humboldt University Berlin largely confirm the ANFI data. Other sources provide very different figures. FAO's Global Forest Resources Assessment (2005) reports a slight overall increase in forest cover from 28.8 percent in 1990 to 28.1 percent in 2000 to 29 percent in 2005. According to World Development Indicators (World Bank 2005), Albania's forest area counted for 36.2 percent of the total land area in 2000 and has decreased by an average of 0.8 percent per year between 1990 and 2000.
6 Coppice is forest originating mainly from shoots or root suckers, often after original trees have been cut.

Chapter 4. Unmaking Socialist Agriculture: The Dissolution of Collective Structures

1 The full title of this law is Law No. 7501 (dated 19 July 1991) "Concerning the Land."
2 The saying plays on a well-known Albanian joke: One day the father-in-law proposes to his wife (*krushka*) to get intimate. The mother-in-law gets angry and slaps him on the cheek. Later that day, the father-in-law gets kicked by his mule (*mushka*). So he got one slap from Krushka and one from Mushka.
3 The ad hoc restitutions occurred despite that fact that the Land Law ordered the organs of local power to prevent any act of land occupation under their jurisdiction (Article 21).
4 The full title of this law is Law No. 9235 (dated 29 July 2004) "On Restitution and Compensation of Property."
5 Many rural Albanians take more balanced positions between the two extremes – full distribution or full restitution. Usually these involve some combination of the two modes of land privatization. One common position is that it would have been best to distribute cooperative land on a per capita basis but give preference to ancestral land.
6 According to the Ministry of Agriculture and Food (2002), food imports rose from US$ 58 million in 1989 to US$ 227 million in 2000. During the same time agricultural exports dropped from US$ 121 million to US$ 29 million.
7 The EU lifted its trade barriers in 1999 under the Autonomous Trade Preferences (ATP). Since then, most Albanian goods have entered the European market without

quotas or custom duties. Regarding agricultural products, fresh goods face quantitative restrictions, but no tariffs and processed goods enter on reduced custom duties. Although for EU standards these terms are quite generous, a number of barriers have been erected that restrict the trade concessions. Complex bureaucratic provisions and the duty to comply with the rigorous technical requirements seem to have replaced border protection (cf. Abdul-Hamid 2003).
8 For examples, see Lusho and Papa (1998), Lemel and Dubali (2000) and Apostoli (2002).
9 In Albanian: *Ta qepemi maleve dhe kodrave ti bëjmë pjellore si fushat!*
10 In Albanian: *Ta bëjmë fshatin si qyteti!*

Chapter 5. Unraveling the Socialist Countryside: Differentiation among Villages and its Effects on Land Use

1 For other cases of disappointment, see de Waal (1995) and de Soto et al. (2002).
2 Unless noted otherwise, all prices, fees and salaries in this book are those paid in 2003/04, assuming an exchange rate of 125 Lek to the Euro.
3 For a detailed account of illegal migration of Albanians to Greece, Italy and other Western European countries, see Nicholson (2002, 439).
4 The minimum legal requirement for school attendance in Albania is 8 years (*shkolla 8-vjeçare*). After this elementary education, students can choose to go on to four years of high school (*shkolla e mesme* or *gjimnaz*) and then to university (*shkolla e lartë* or *universitet*).
5 IFA-trucks are light, four-wheel drive vehicles that were produced by a conglomerate of companies (*Industrieverband Fahrzeugbau*) in East Germany until the early 1990s. They are the most popular truck used in Albania (see Photo 1.2).
6 Mal i Thatë means "Dry Mountain" in English.
7 The one exception to this general rule was olives, but olives were not produced in Dardha.
8 Although wages in Greece were much higher than in Macedonia, far fewer households chose to go there. The main reason for this was that at the beginning of the 1990s, wages in Macedonia were on a par with those in Greece. Therefore workers from Dardha naturally gravitated towards Macedonia, which was closer, where they already spoke the language, and where they suffered less discrimination than in Greece. Over the course of the 1990s, however, the situation changed. While Greece experienced an economic boom, wages in Macedonia decreased. It also became more difficult to find work in Macedonia. By 2004, workers from Dardha found it very difficult to get to Greece. Without a long-standing history of employment, they were unable to obtain working visas and, even more importantly, could not establish connections to Greek employers.
9 In his famous book "The Isolated State", first published in 1826, von Thünen sought to explain the principles that govern the location of rural land use around a market town. In the book, von Thünen constructed a model of what he believed to be the most efficient spatial layout of rural land use. Based on the simplified assumption that all land is a uniform, flat plain of equal soil quality and climate, von Thünen postulated a geographical pattern with concentric rings, or zones, around the market center. The first ring, the one nearest to the market, was devoted to gardening and milk

production; the second ring to forestry (for fuel and timber); the third to an intensive crop rotation system (without fallow); the fourth to an "improved" system of crop farming, fallow and pasture; the fifth to a three-field system; and finally, the sixth to livestock production. The last ring was at the farthest extremity of production. Here land rent was zero because the cost of transporting products to the market had become too high. The marginal cost of going the additional distance had exceeded the market price of the product. Although von Thünen's considerably simplified the "real world," his model tends to hold true in most instances. For applications of von Thünen's ideas on a wide range of spatial scales, see, for example, Chisholm (1962), Peet (1969), and Blaikie (1971a,b).

10 See Chapter 6 for a thorough analysis of household capital and labor allocation.

11 Income from off-farm sources includes income from wages, salaries and off-farm self-employment. It also comprises income from seasonal labor migration, which is substantial in the case of Dardha.

Chapter 6. The Crisis of Capital and Labor: Effects on Land Use within Villages

1 The banks' policies regarding small credit, however, are about to change significantly. A few large Albanian banks have recently discovered smallholders as potential customers. Many of them now offer credit to farmers without asking for high collateral. For example, one of Albania's largest banks, ProCredit Bank, offers Agricultural Credit (*Kredi Bujqësore*) for up to 24,000 Euro without encumbering farmers with a mortgage.

2 Regarding cattle, the differences among households were less striking. On average, the 56 households (for which I have income data) owned 1.2 cows. The richest owned 1.4 and the poorest owned 1.3.

3 For example, households with one or more members in a political position, on average planted less wheat and corn and kept less sheep and goats than households without access to political authority. At the same time, they used about the same amount of land and produced slightly more grapes. Similarly, a household's past experience with agriculture did not correlate with its land use outputs. Households in which the head of the household worked in the agricultural sector during socialism, produced more grapes and small ruminants than households in which the head of the household had worked in industry or the service sector. Yet, at the same time, the latter planted more grain and used about the same amount of land. Finally, access to social networks, such as farmers'-, credit-, tourism-, and cultural associations, and political parties, led to varying results regarding production outcomes. Households that had members in many networks tended to produce more grapes and less sheep and goats than households that had members in few networks. Yet, unlike with access to capital and labor, a correlation between network membership, on the one hand, and wheat and corn cultivation and overall production area, on the other, did not exist.

4 The selling prices quoted here for grapes, onions and tomatoes refer to gross turnover. To calculate profits, expenses such as the costs of water, fertilizer, pesticides and fungicides have to be subtracted.

5 In total, I conducted 74 household interviews in the three villages. Of these, only 53 allowed for the combination of income, labor and land use data.

Chapter 7. The Fate of the Postsocialist Forest

1. DGFP et al. (2002), FAO (2005) and INSTAT (2005).
2. Cf. de Waal (2004), Bemmann and Große (2001) and Ministry of Agriculture and Food (2002).
3. I am referring to Law No. 7623 (dated 13 October 1992) 'Concerning Forests and the Forest Service Police'. The stipulations regarding infringement of its provisions are updated in Law No. 7838 (dated 30 June 1994).
4. Cf. Legisi 2001, cited in de Waal 2004:35.
5. When I asked a forest officer in 2004 why the District Forest Service at the time encouraged de facto forest restitution, he pointed to the low value of Kodra's forest resources and to the Service's chronic lack of staff. "Technically", he said, "it was not even forest […] most of it was cut". Furthermore, he explained, the Service had been "too busy" with the protection of other forest areas.
6. Within Kodra, the distribution of these benefits is relatively egalitarian. Although households possess different areas of chestnut forest, the differences in benefits were small and relatively insignificant in relation to the overall household income which, in 2004, was 4,390 Euro on average.
7. The full title of this legislation is "Regulation No. 308 (dated 26 January 1996) 'On the Transfer of Forest and Pastures in Use to Communes' ".
8. In addition, many villagers from Dardha explain the decision for a communal arrangement with pressure from powerful actors at the commune. These actors, villagers believe, were pushing for a communal rather than an individual arrangement because they realized that by controlling access to the communal forest, they could capture rents in form of political power and/or monetary benefits.
9. The chairpersons of the village commissions, in turn, were elected in each village by the association members, i.e. all communal forest users (cf. CFPM/SNV 2003).
10. The commune administration and the donor agencies also have their say in this.
11. According to Law No. 7838 (dated 30 June 1994), infringements of the legal stipulations of Law No. 7623, which are not criminal offences and which have caused a damage of less than 400 Euro, are punished as administrative infringements with an indemnification of the damage and a fine ranging from 40 to 400 Euro. The tools used to carry out the damage and the extracted forest products are confiscated and pass into government ownership. If the damage of the infringement is more than 400 Euro the perpetrator will be charged according to the provisions of the Criminal Code of Albania.

BIBLIOGRAPHY

Abdul-Hamid, Yara. 2003. *A Fair Deal For Albanian Farmers. Oxfam Briefing Paper 45*. Oxford: Oxfam.
Apostoli, Stilian. 2002. *Prespa. Zhvillime Social-Ekonomike. [Prespa. Socio-Economic Development]*. Tirana: Flesh.
Bemmann, Albrecht and Werner Große. 2001. "Waldeigentumsveränderungen in Mittel- Und Osteuropäischen Transformationsländern." *Allgemeine Forst- und Jagdzeitung* 172:173–83.
Berry, Sara. 1993. *No Condition Is Permanent: The Social Dynamics of Agrarian Change in Sub-Saharan Africa*. Madison: University of Wisconsin Press.
Biberaj, Elez. *Albania in Transition. The Rocky Road to Democracy*. San Francisco: Westview Press.
Blaikie, Piers. 1985. *The Political Economy of Soil Erosion in Developing Countries*. New York: Longman.
———. 1971a. "Spatial Organization of Agriculture in Some North Indian Villages: Part I." *Transaction of the Institute of British Geographers* 52:1–40.
———. 1971b. "Spatial Organization of Agriculture in Some North Indian Villages: Part II." *Transaction of the Institute of British Geographers* 53:15–3.
Blaikie, Piers and Harold Brookfield. 1987. *Land Degradation and Society*. London, New York: Methuen.
Bromley, Daniel W. 1991. *Environment and Economy. Property Rights and Public Policy*. Oxford, Cambridge: Blackwell.
Brubaker, Rogers, Margit Feischmidt, Jon Fox, and Liana Grancea. 2006. *Nationalist Politics and Everyday Ethnicity in a Transylvanian Town*. Princeton: Princeton University Press.
Bryant, Raymond and Sinead L. Bailey. 1997. *Third World Political Ecology*. New York: Routledge.
Carletto, Calogero, Benjamin Davis, Marco Stampini, and Alberto Zezza. 2006. "A Country on the Move: Internal Mobility and International Migration in Post-Communist Albania." *International Migration Review* 40(4):767–85.
CFPM/SNV. 2003. *Communal Forests and Pastures Management. Case Studies*. Peshkopi, Albania: CFPM/SNV.
Chisholm, Michael. 1962. *Rural Settlement and Land Use. An Essay in Location*. London: Hutchinson University Press.
Cungu, Azeta and Johan F. M. Swinnen. 1999. "Albania's Radical Agrarian Reforms." *Economic Development and Cultural Change* 47(3):605–19.
De Rapper, Gilles. 2005. "Better Than Muslims, Not As Good As Greeks: Emigration As Experienced and Imagined by the Albanian Christians of Lunxhëri." Pp. 173–94 in *The New Albanian Migration*, Editors Russell King, Nicola Mai, and Stephanie Schwandner-Sievers. Brighton: University of Sussex Press.

De Soto, Hermine G., Peter Gordon, Ilir Gedeshi, and Zamira Sinoimeri. 2002. *Poverty in Albania. A Qualitative Assessment*. World Bank Technical Paper No. 520. Washington, D.C.: World Bank.

De Waal, Clarissa. 2004. "Post-Socialist Property Rights and Wrongs in Albania. An Ethnography of Agrarian Change." *Conservation and Society* 2(1):19–50.

———. 1995. "Decollectivisation and Total Scarcity in High Albania." *Cambridge Anthropology* 18(1):1–22.

Deere, Carmen D. and Alain De Janvry. 1979. "A Conceptual Framework for the Empirical Analysis of Peasantries." *American Journal of Agricultural Economics* (November):601–11.

DGFP, FAO, WFP, and SNV. 2002. *Effects of the Albania Forestry Project on Poverty Reduction*. Tirana: Directorate General of Forests and Pastures.

Fakiolas, Rossetos. 2003. "Regularising Undocumented Immigrants in Greece: Procedures and Effects." *Journal of Ethnic and Migration Studies* 29(3):535–61.

Fetter, Frank. 1977. *Capital, Interest, and Rent: Essays in the Theory of Distribution*. Kansas City: Sheed Andrews and McMeel.

Fine, Ben. 1979. "On Marx's Theory of Agricultural Rent." *Economy and Society* 8(3):231–78.

Food and Agricultural Organization. 2006. FAOSTAT. Online: http://faostat.fao.org (accessed 1 February 2006).

———. 2005. Forest Resources Assessment. Online: http://www.fao.org/forestry/foris/webview/forestry2/index.jsp?siteId=4961&sitetreeId=22052&langId=1&geoId=144 (accessed 25 April 2006).

Giordano, Christian and Dobrinka Kostova. 2002. "The Social Production of Mistrust." Pp. 74–91 in *Postsocialism. Ideals, Ideologies and Practices in Eurasia*, Editor Christopher Hann. London: Routledge.

GSHDNJ (Grupi Shqiptar i të Drejtave të Njeriut). 2003. *Minoritetet: E Tashmja Dhe e Ardhmja. Raport i GSHDNJ Mbi Situatën e Pakicave Në Shqipëri. Minorities: The Present and the Future. Report of AHRG on the Situation of Minorities in Albania*. Tirana: Botimet "Kanun".

Gustafson, Ingrid. 2003. *Young Dreams. Success Strategies of Girls in South-East Albania*. Unpublished Master's Thesis. Stockholm University, Department of Social Anthropology.

Guthman, Julie. 2004a. *Agrarian Dreams. The Paradox of Organic Farming in California*. Berkeley: University of California Press.

———. 2004b. "Back to the Land: The Paradox of Organic Food Standards." *Environment and Planning A* 36:511–28.

Hann, Christopher. 1993. "From Production to Property: Decollectivization and the Family-Land Relationship in Contemporary Hungary." *Man* 28(2):299–320.

Hardin, Garrett. 1968. " The Tragedy of the Commons." *Science* 162:1243–48.

Harvey, David. 1982. *Limits to Capital*. Chicago: University of Chicago Press.

Hashi, Iraj and Lindita Xhillari. 1999. "Privatisation and Transition in Albania." *Post-Communist Economies* 11(1):99–125.

Hecht, Susanna. 1985. "Environment, Development and Politics: Capital Accumulation and the Livestock Sector in Eastern Amazonia." *World Development* 13(6):663–84.

Humphrey, Caroline. 1983. *Karl Marx Collective: Economy, Society and Religion in a Siberian Collective Farm*. Cambridge: Cambridge University Press.

INSTAT. 2005. *Shqipëria Në Shifra. Albania in Figures*. Tirana: Instituti i Statistikës.

Jarvis, Christopher. 2000. "The Rise and Fall of Albania's Pyramid Schemes." *Finance and Development* 37(1).

Kaneff, Deema. 1998. "When 'Land' Becomes 'Territory'." Pp. 16–32 in *Surviving Post-Socialism. Local Strategies and Regional Responses in Eastern Europe and the Former Soviet Union*, Editors S Bridger and Francis Pine. London: Routledge.

Kelly, Ellen. 2005. "Lifestyles and Integration of Albanian Women in Bologna: Two Steps Forward, One Step Back?" Pp. 29–63 in *The New Albanian Migration*, Editors Russell King, Nicola Mai, and Stephanie Schwandner-Sievers. Brighton: University of Sussex Press.

King, Russell. 2005. "Albania As a Laboratory for the Study of Migration and Development." *Journal of Southern Europe and the Balkans* 7(2):133–55.

King, Russell and Steve Burton. 1982. "Land Fragmentation: Notes on a Fundamental Rural Spatial Problem." *Progress in Human Geography* 6(4):475–94.

King, Russell and Julie Vullnetari. 2003. *Migration and Development in Albania*. Working Paper C5. Brighton: Sussex Centre for Migration Research.

Kodderitzsch, Severin. 1999. *Reforms in Albanian Agriculture. Assessing a Sector in Transition*. World Bank Technical Paper No. 431. World Bank.

Konidaris, Gerasimos. 2005. "Examining Policy Responses to Immigration in the Light of Interstate Relations and Foreign Policy Objectives: Greece and Albania." Pp. 64–92 in *The New Albanian Migration*, Editors Russell King, Nicola Mai, and Stephanie Schwandner-Sievers. Brighton: University of Sussex Press.

Kornai, János. 1980. *Economics of Shortage*. Amsterdam: North Holland Publishers.

Lampland, Martha. 2002. "The Advantages of Being Collectivized: Cooperative Farm Managers in the Postsocialist Economy." Pp. 31–56 in *Postsocialism. Ideals, Ideologies and Practices in Eurasia*, Editor Christopher Hann. London: Routledge.

Leach, Melissa, Robin Mearns, and Ian Scoones. 1999. "Environmental Entitlements: Dynamics and Institutions in Community-Based Natural Resource Management." *World Development* 27(2):225–47.

Lemel, Harold (ed.). 2000. *Rural Property and Economy in Post-Communist Albania*. New York, Oxford: Berghahn Books.

———. 1999. "A Glimpse of Change in Albania's Post-Communist Countryside." *Quarterly Journal of International Agriculture* 38(1):21–43.

———. 1998. "Rural Land Privatisation and Distribution in Albania: Evidence From the Field." *Europe-Asia Studies* 50(1):121–40.

Lemel, Harold and Albert Dubali. 2000. "Land Fragmentation." Pp. 109–26 in *Rural Property and Economy in Post-Communist Albania*, editor Harold Lemel. New York, Oxford: Berghahn Books.

Lerman, Zvi. 2001. "Agriculture in Transition Economies: From Common Heritage to Divergence." *Agricultural Economics* 26:95–114.

Lusho, Sherif and Dhimiter Papa. 1998. *Land Fragmentation and Consolidation in Albania*. Working Paper No. 25. Madison: Land Tenure Center, University of Wisconsin.

Macours, Karen and Johan F. M. Swinnen. 2002. "Patterns of Transition." *Economic Development and Cultural Change* 50(3):365–94.

Malinowski, Bronislaw. 1922. *Argonauts of the Western Pacific*. London.

Marx, Karl. 2003. *Das Kapital. Dritter Band: Der Gesamtprozess der kapitalistischen Produktion*. [Original 1894]. Berlin: Dietz.

Mathijs, Erik. 1997. "An Historical Overview of Central and Eastern European Land Reform." Pp. 33–53 in *Political Economy of Agrarian Reform in Central and Eastern Europe*, Editor Johan F. M. Swinnen. Aldershot: Ashgate.

Meta, Mehmet. 1993. "Forests and Forest Policy in Albania." *Journal of Forestry* 91(6):27–28.

Miluka, Juna, Gero Carletto, Benjamin Davis, and Alberto Zezza. 2007. *The Vanishing Farms? The Impact of International Migration on Albanian Family Farming*. Policy Research Working Paper 4367. World Bank.

Ministry of Agriculture and Food. 2002. *Annual Report.* Tirana, Albania: Ministry of Agriculture and Food.

Mises, Ludwig v. 1961. *Human Action: A Treatise on Economics.* New Haven: Yale University Press.

Moore, Donald. 1993. "Contesting Terrain in Zimbabwe's Eastern Highlands: Political Ecology, Ethnography, and Peasant Resource Struggles." *Economic Geography* 69(4):380–401.

Müller, Daniel and Björn Wode. 2003. Manual on Participatory Village Mapping Using Photomaps. Trainer Guide. Social Forestry Development Project. Son Da, Vietnam.

Nicholson, Beryl. 2004. "Migrants As Agents of Development: Albanian Return Migrants and Micro-Enterprise." Pp. 94–110 in *New Patterns of Labour Migration in Central and Eastern Europe*, Editor D Pop. Cluj Napoca, Romania: AMM Editura.

———. 2002. "The Wrong End of the Telescope: Economic Migrants, Immigration Policy, and How It Looks From Albania." *The Political Quarterly* 73(4):436–44.

Olsen, Neil. 2000. *Albania. An Oxfam Country Profile.* Oxford: Oxfam.

Ostrom, Elinor. 1990. *Governing the Commons. The Evolution of Institutions for Collective Action.* Cambridge: Cambridge University Press.

Paasch, Rolf. 2003. "Angebot, Nachfrage Und Gottes Ratschlag. Die albanischen Bauern haben schwer mit der Agrarpolitik der Europäischen Union zu kämpfen." *Frankfurter Rundschau. 10 September 2003.* Frankfurt.

Peet, Richard. 1969. "The Spatial Expansion of Commercial Agriculture in the Nineteenth Century: A Von Thunen Interpretation." *Economic Geography* 45(4):283–301.

Peet, Richard and Michael E. Watts. 1996. *Liberation Ecologies : Environment, Development, Social Movements.* London, New York: Routledge.

Peluso, Nancy L. 1992. *Rich Forests, Poor People: Resource Control and Resistance in Java.* Berkeley: University of California Press.

Perry, Duncan M. 1997. "The Republic of Macedonia: Finding Its Way." Pp. 226–81 in *Politics, Power, and the Struggle for Democracy in South-East Europe*, Editors Karen Dawisha and Bruce Parrott. Cambridge: Cambridge University Press.

Pettifer, James. 2001. *Albania & Kosovo. Blue Guide.* London: A & C Black.

Pettifer, James and Miranda Vickers. 2007. *The Albanian Question. Reshaping the Balkans.* London, New York: I.B. Tauris.

Ribot, Jesse C. 1998. "Theorizing Access: Forest Profits Along Senegal's Charcoal Commodity Chain." *Development and Change* 29:307–41.

Ribot, Jesse C. and Nancy L. Peluso. 2003. "A Theory of Access." *Rural Sociology* 68(2):153–81.

Ricardo, David. 1973. *The Principles of Political Economy and Taxation.* [Original 1817]. London: Everyman's Library.

Saltmarshe, Douglas. 2001. *Identity in a Post-Communist Balkan State. An Albanian Village Study.* Aldershot, Burlington: Ashgate.

———. 2000. "Local Government in Practice. Evidence From Two Villages in Northern Albania." *Public Administration and Development* (20):327–37.

Schwandner-Sievers, Stephanie. 1999. *The Albanian Aromanians' Awakening: Identity Politics and Conflicts in Post-Communist Albania.* ECMI Working Paper No.3. Flensburg: European Centre for Minority Issues.

Scott, James C. 1985. *Weapons of the Weak: Everyday Forms of Peasant Resistance.* New Haven: Yale University Press.

———. 1976. *The Moral Economy of the Peasant.* New Haven: Yale University Press.

Sikor, Thomas. 2006. "Land As Asset, Land As Liability: Property Politics in Rural Central and Eastern Europe." *Changing Properties of Property*, Editors Franz v. Benda-Beckmann, Keebet v. Benda-Beckmann, and Melanie Wiber. New York: Berghahn.

Sjöberg, Örjan. 1991. *Rural Change and Development in Albania*. Oxford, San Francisco: Westview Press.

Swinnen, Johan F. M., Allan Buckwell, and Erik Mathijs. 1997. *Agricultural Privatisation, Land Reform and Farm Restructuring in Central and Eastern Europe*. Aldershot: Ashgate.

Swinnen, Johan F. M. (Editor). 1997. *Political Economy of Agrarian Reform in Central and Eastern Europe*. Aldershot: Ashgate.

Thelen, Tatjana. 2003. *Privatisierung und soziale Ungleichheit in der osteuropäischen Landwirtschaft. Zwei Fallstudien aus Ungarn und Rumänien*. Frankfurt, New York: Campus.

Thünen, Johann H. v. 1966. *The Isolated State*. [Original 1826]. Oxford: Pergamon Press.

To, Phuc X. and Thomas Sikor. 2009 "The Politics of Illegal Logging in Vietnam." Under Review at *Society and Natural Resources*.

Tribe, Keith. 1977. "Economic Property and the Theorisation of Ground Rent." *Economy and Society* 6(1):69–88.

Verdery, Katherine. 2004. "The Obligations of Ownership: Restoring Rights to Land in Postsocialist Transylvania." Pp. 139–60 in *Property in Question: Value Transformation in the Global Economy*, Editors Katherine Verdery and Caroline Humphrey. Oxford: Berg Press.

———. 2003. *The Vanishing Hectare: Property and Value in Postsocialist Transylvania*. Ithaca, N.Y.: Cornell University Press.

———. 1999. "Fuzzy Property: Rights, Power, and Identity in Transylvania's Decollectivization." Pp. 53–81 in *Uncertain Transition. Ethnographies of Change in the Postsocialist World*, Editors Michael Burawoy and Katherine Verdery. Boulder, New York, Oxford: Rowman & Littlefield.

———. 1998. "Property and Power in Transylvania's Decollectivization." Pp. 160–180 in *Property Relations. Renewing the Anthropological Tradition*, Editor Christopher Hann. Cambridge, UK: Cambridge University Press.

Vickers, Miranda and James Pettifer. 1997. *Albania: From Anarchy to a Balkan Identity*. London: Hurst and Company.

Voell, Stéphane. 2003. "The Kanun in the City. Albanian Customary Law As a Habitus and Its Persistence in the Suburb of Tirana, Bathore." *Anthropos* 98:85–101.

Watts, Michael. 1983. *Silent Violence. Food, Famine & Peasantry in Northern Nigeria*. Berkeley: University of California Press.

Winnifrith, Tom J. 1987. *The Vlachs: The History of a Balkan People*. London: Duckworth.

Woodcock, Shannon. 2007. "The Absence of Albanian Jokes About Socialism, Or Why Some Dictatorships Are Not Funny." Pp. 51–68 in *The Politics and Aesthetics of Refusal*, Editors Caroline Hamilton et al. Cambridge: Cambridge Scholars Press.

World Bank. 2005. World Development Indicators. Online: http://devdata.worldbank.org/wdi2005/Section3.htm (accessed 25 April 2006).

Zbierski-Salameh, Slawomira. 1999. "Polish Peasants in the "Valley of Transition": Responses to Postsocialist Reforms." Pp. 189–222 in *Uncertain Transition. Ethnographies of Change in the Postsocialist World*, Editors Michael Burawoy and Katherine Verdery. Lanham, Boulder, Oxford: Rowman & Littlefield.

Zezza, Alberto, Gero Carletto, and Benjamin Davis. 2005. "Moving Away From Poverty: A Spatial Analysis of Poverty and Migration in Albania." *Journal of Southern Europe and the Balkans* 7(2):175–93.

INDEX

access: definition 10; land use and 56–59; political ecology views on 11–12; as tool for control 7–10. *see also* rent
agricultural production: associations for 63; capital access and 87–88; equipment 82; factors influencing 81–83; infrastructure for 62; labor shortages and 86–88; pollution from 34; subsistence farming 59–62; success stories 88–90; trade liberalization and 59–62; village efforts 36–37, 66, 69, 71, 72
Albania: break with USSR 16, 20; and European Union 119–120; European Union and 59; as first atheist state 17; forecasts for 120; isolationist problems 16–17; labor camps 17; land laws 47–48, 56, 100–101; leaders of 16, 17–18, 22; postsocialism conditions 3, 5, 38, 41–42, 55–56, 59–60; revolt against socialism 22–24; as socialist country 3, 15–27, 18, 19–22; travel in 1–3
Alia, Ramiz 22
assets, village 77–78

Bagëtia: agricultural production 36–37, 69; assets 77–78; biophysical conditions 75–76; capital access 84–86; ethnic populations 26, 73–74; extensification in 36–40, 69–70; family stories 89–91, 109–110; forests 41–42, 97–99, 109–116; housing 85; income 70, 76–77, 84, 114–115; infrastructure 77–78; irrigation systems 32; labor shortages 86–87; land use 30, 39–41, **44**, 52–54, 73–74; livestock 37, 70; market access 69–70, 74–75; migration from 70, 73–74; political power in 78–79; population 69; postsocialism conditions 65–66; as socialist community 25, 26–27; waste disposal 34
biophysical conditions: climate 61; grape growing 95; impact on land use 75–76; industrial pollution 34; soil erosion 32–34; terraces 32–34, 63; waste disposal 34, **35,** 63; watershed contamination 34
Bulgaria 9, 10

capital access 9–10, 82, 84–93
chestnut forests 41, 101–103
climate conditions 61
collectives and collectivism: break up of 29; building rural infrastructure 62; postsocialism 63–64; redistribution of land 47–48; under socialism 18–19
Compensation Law 56
control and access 7–10
credit, use of 85
credit associations 63–64, 85

Dardha: agricultural production 37, 71, 72; assets 77–78; biophysical conditions 75–76; capital access 84–86; distance to land plots 60–61; ethnic populations 26, 73–74; extensification 37, 38, 70–72; family stories 91–92, 104–105; field management **1,** 61; forest and pasture user association 106–108; forests 41–42, 103–108; grape growing 37; housing 85; income 72, 76–77, 84; infrastructure 77–78;

Dardha: (*Continued*)
irrigation systems **31,** 32; labor shortages 86–87; land use 30, 40–41, **45,** 49–51, **54,** 73–74, **93**; market access 71, 74–75; migration from 71–72; political power in 78–79; population 70–71; as socialist community 25–27; terraces 32–34; waste disposal 34, 63
Dautovski, Rako 106–108
distance to land plots 60–61
Drini family 102–103
Dulellari, Maks 52–53, 109–110

education and labor supply 87
emigration. *see* migration
ethnicity: as control mechanism 10; discrimination and 67–68, 70–72; impact on land use 73–74; in villages 26, 73–74
Europe, Central and Eastern 4–5
European Union (EU) 59, 119–120
extensification: Bagëtia 36–40, 69–70; Dardha 37, 40, 70–72; definition 34; intra-village patterns 40–41; reasons for 38, 117–118; spatial factors 93–95

farms and farming. *see* agricultural production
finances. *see* capital access
Forest Law 100–101
forests: associations for 106–108; chestnut trees 41, 101–103; degradation of 41–42, 118; government control of 100–101, 110–111, 113–114; illegal harvesting 97–99, 109–110; income from 114–116; as national resource 99; ownership of 100–101; Qafë Panje and Guri Nikes 41, 97–99, 109–116; restitution to original owners 100, 102–103; use conflicts 110–114; vandalism 101–105. *see also* logging

Geri family 90–91, 94
goods and services access 3–4, 6–10
grain production 36, 82

grape growing 36, 37, 63, 69, 82–84, 95
Greece 67–68, 70

Heifer Project International (HPI) 63
housing 85
Hoxha, Enver 16, 17–18
Hoxha, Gjergji 97–99, 113–115
Hungary 8–9, 9

immigration laws 67–68, 70
income: Bagëtia 70, 84, 114–116; Dardha 72, 84; Kodra 68–69, 84, 103; sources of 76–77
infrastructure, village 62, 77–78
intensification: definition 34; intra-village patterns 40–41; Kodra 36, 39, 66–69; reasons for 38, 117–118; spatial factors 93–95
investments 85–86
irrigation systems 30–32, 36, 62–63
Italy 67–68

Kodra: agricultural production 36, 66, 69; assets 77–78; biophysical conditions 75–76; capital access 84–86; credit association 63–64, 85; crop production 36, 69; ethnic populations 26, 73–74; family stories 88–90, 102–103, 114; farmers' associations 63, 85; field management 61; forests 41–42, 101–103; housing 85; income 68–69, 76–77, 84; infrastructure 77–78; intensification in land use 36, 38, 66–69; irrigation systems 32, 36; labor shortages 86–87; land use **30,** 39–41, **43,** 48–49, **54,** 73–74, 83–84; livestock 36, 69; market access 74–75; migration from 67–68; political power in 78–79; population size 66; postsocialism conditions 65–66; small businesses in 68; as socialist community 24–25, 26–27; terrace destruction 32–34; waste disposal 34, **35**

labor supply: agricultural production and 82, 87–88; as control mechanism 9;

shortages 86–87; significance of 92–93; stories about 88–93. *see also* migration
land commissions 48–51
Land Law 47–54
land use: advantages of diversified plots 59–62; biophysical conditions 61, 75–76; consolidation failures 55–56, 59–62; distribution 48–51, 56–59; ethnicity and 73–74; extensification 34, 93–95, 117–118; fragmentation of 29, **54,** 60–62, 117; intensification 34, 93–95, 117–118; land commissions 48–51; laws of 47–48, 56, 100–101; market access impacts 74–75; rental 93–95; restitution 52–54; risk management 61; spatial factors 6, 34, 93–95; and subsistence farming 59–62. *see also* agricultural production; forests; rent
livestock: Bagëtia 37, 70; collective herding 64; Heifer Project International 63; investment needed for 82; Kodra 36, 69
logging 97–99, 103, 110–116. *see also* forests

Macedonia 67–68, 71–72
market access 4, 9, 69–71, 74–75
Meksi family 90–91, 94
migration: Bagëtia 70, 73–74; Dardha 71–72, 73–74; EU membership impact on 120; Kodra 67–68, 73–74; return of 120. *see also* labor supply

onion growing 36

plot structures 30, 60–61
political ecology and rent 6–7, 11–12, 119
political power, village 78–79

pollution 34
population, village 66, 69–71
property rights and access control 8–9
pyramid investment schemes 55

Qafë Panje and Guri Nikes forests 41, 97–99, 109–116

raki production 7–8
rent: as access control 56–59; agreements 83–84; as analytical tool 3–4, 6, 117–119; land use change and 56–59, 117–119; political ecology and 6–7, 11–12, 119; spatial factors in 6, 93–95. *see also* access
restitution of land 52–54
risk management 61
Romania 9–10

Sherifi family 82, 83–84, 88–90, 94, 114
Shkurtaj family 115
Shumka family 91–92, 94, 104–105
social networks 9, 58
soil erosion 32–34
subsistence farming 59–62

terraces 32–34, 63
trade markets 59–60, 71, 110–115

values of resources 10–12
vandalism: forests 101–105, 109; irrigation systems 30, 32; over land distribution 58; resulting from financial crisis 55–56; during socialist revolt 24

waste disposal 34, **35,** 63
watershed contamination 34

Zela, Bashkim 83, 114